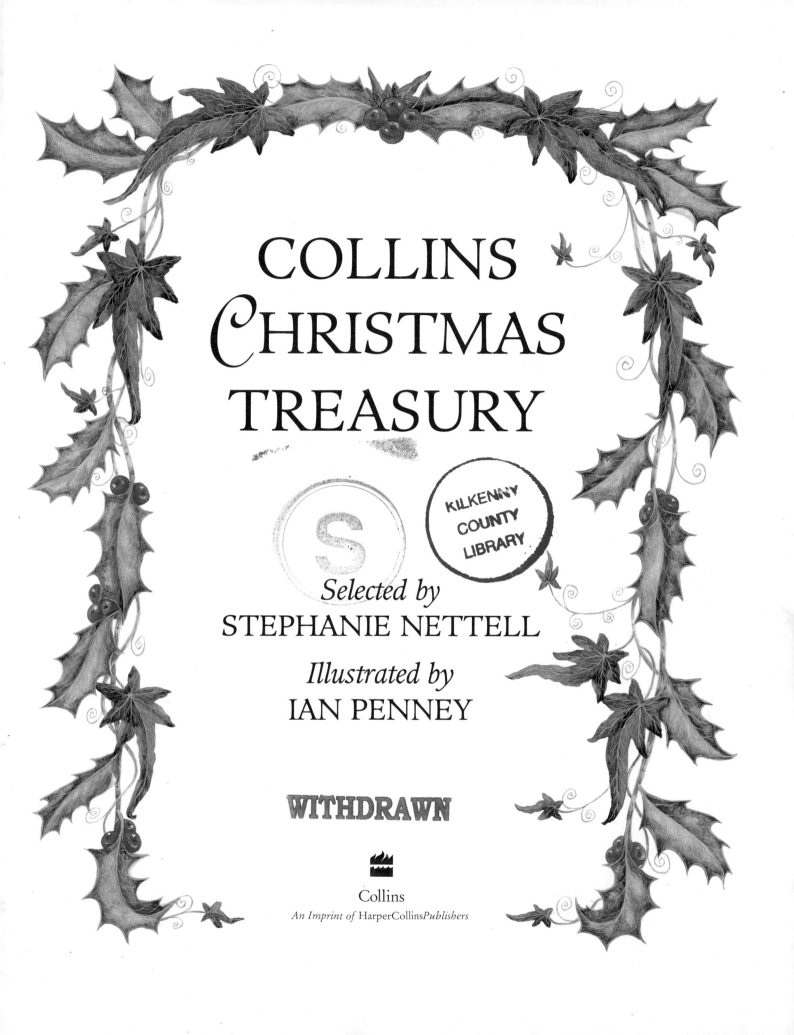

COLLINS
CHRISTMAS
TREASURY

Selected by
STEPHANIE NETTELL

Illustrated by
IAN PENNEY

Collins
An Imprint of HarperCollinsPublishers

For Margaret and Keith
IP
To Gina Pollinger, gratefully
SN

First published in Great Britain by HarperCollins Publishers Ltd in 1996
1 3 5 7 9 10 8 6 4 2
ISBN: 0 00 198057 2
Compilation copyright © Stephanie Nettell 1996
Illustration copyright © Ian Penney 1996

CONTENTS

INTRODUCTION

I've always felt that on the long shelf of Christmas books there was still room for a *family* anthology, one that adults could enjoy but also share with children of all ages. One that mixed the familiar, the unexpected and the completely new. One which both young and old could dip into and exclaim: "I've never known the actual words to that!" or, "Do you remember that lovely bit when...?" or simply, "Oh, *that's* a good one."

The excitement of Christmas begins as soon as a baby is hypnotised by a sparkly tree, and seems to affect people of every faith and no faith. We never entirely grow out of it – all our lives we remember *exactly* the mysterious crackling of a heavy stocking. The opening chords of a carol, the smell of plum pudding... and we're six years old again.

The spirit of Christmas is universal. Pioneers and refugees, missionaries and soldiers have carried it, in hope or homesickness, to lands far from their childhood. In this collection I've tried to show how Christmas stirs us all, even in despair – a reminder, when we're warm and fed and surrounded by love, that it is Christmas, too, for those who have nothing, who are lonely perhaps, or even at war.

Here, in their own words, people remember Christmas wherever they are – on a midsummer beach under the fluffy red blooms of a pohutukawa tree or trudging through snow beneath dark fir trees – and whatever time they lived – from Armenia a thousand years ago to twentieth-century Wales. These are poems and stories to celebrate the way Christmas lifts our spirits and brings us together the world over.

Stephanie Nettell

A CHILD IS BORN

THE CHRIST CHILD

His aquamarine eyes have opened
the smiling sea of morning.
Two lightning suns have opened the dawn.

His pomegranate cheeks are pink flowers
of the laurel, the pink flowers
through which stem and roots
greet man's sight with love.

His smooth arms reach,
making a harmonious, symmetrical arch,
to hold up the world.

His mouth a double petal rose,
his tongue a sweet voiced harp,
his hair adorned with rosemary,
in triple braids, shines with light.

His wrists, bouquets of violets.
And when he breathes
incense fills the room,
incense with divine fire.

When he walks it will be
as if vermilion, blue and gold
brocades, belted with silver
woven with stones, will move.

Eternal glory to Him,
newly born saviour, the king.
And to the One Who adorns Him.

Krikor Naregatsi (951-1003)

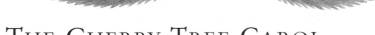

THE CHERRY TREE CAROL

An Appalachian Folk Song

As Joseph and Mary were a-walking the green,
They was apples and cherries plenty there to be seen.

And then Mary said to Joseph, so meek and so mild:
Gather me some cherries, Joseph, for I am with child.

Then Joseph said to Mary so rough and unkind:
Let the daddy of the baby get the cherries for thine.

Then the baby spoke out of its mother's womb:
Bow down you lofty cherry trees, let my mammy have some.

Then the cherry tree bent and it bowed like a bow,
So that Mary picked cherries from the uppermost bough.

Then Joseph took Mary all on his left knee,
Saying: Lord have mercy on me and what I have done.

Then Joseph took Mary on his right knee,
Saying: O my little Saviour, when your birthday shall be,
The hills and high mountains shall bow unto thee.

Then the baby spoke out of its mother's womb:
On old Christmas morning my birthday shall be,
When the hills and high mountains shall bow unto me.

Anon

7

CHRISTMAS LANDSCAPE

Tonight the wind gnaws
with teeth of glass,
the jackdaw shivers
in caged branches of iron,
the stars have talons.

There is hunger in the mouth
of vole and badger,
silver agonies of breath
in the nostril of the fox,
ice on the rabbit's paw.

Tonight has no moon,
no food for the pilgrim;
the fruit tree is bare,
the rose bush a thorn
and the ground is bitter with stones.

But the mole sleeps, and the hedgehog
lies curled in a womb of leaves,
the bean and the wheat-seed
hug their germs in the earth
and the stream moves under the ice.

Tonight there is no moon,
but a new star opens
like a silver trumpet over the dead.
Tonight in a nest of ruins
the blessèd babe is laid.

And the fir tree warms to a bloom of candles,
the child lights his lantern,
stares at his tinselled toy;
our hearts and hearths
smoulder with live ashes.

In the blood of our grief
the cold earth is suckled,
in our agony the womb
convulses its seed,
in the cry of anguish
the child's first breath is born.

Laurie Lee

O SIMPLICITAS

An angel came to me
And I was unprepared
To be what God was using.
Mother I was to be.
A moment I despaired,
Thought briefly of refusing.
The angel knew I heard.
According to God's Word
I bowed to this strange choosing.

A palace should have been
The birthplace of a king
(I had no way of knowing).
We went to Bethlehem;
It was so strange a thing.
The wind was cold, and blowing,
My cloak was old, and thin.
They turned us from the inn;
The town was overflowing.

God's Word, a child so small,
Who still must learn to speak,
Lay in humiliation.
Joseph stood, strong and tall.
The beasts were warm and meek
And moved with hesitation.
The Child born in a stall?
I understood it: all.
Kings came in adoration.

Perhaps it was absurd:
The stable set apart,
The sleepy cattle lowing;
And the incarnate Word
Resting against my heart.
My joy was overflowing.
The shepherds came, adored
The folly of the Lord,
Wiser than all men's knowing.

Madeleine L'Engle

A MAGIC MAID

I saw a sweet, a seemly sight,
A magic maid, a blossom bright,
　　To grief and gladness she gave tongue;
A maiden mother meek and mild
In cradle keeps a small boy-child,
　　That softly slept; she sat and sung,
　　　　Lullay, lulla baloo,
　　　　My bairn, sleep softly noo.

Anon, 1410, adapted

A SINGING IN THE AIR

A snowy field! A stable piled
With straw! A donkey's sleepy pow!
A Mother beaming on a Child!
A Manger, and a munching cow!
– These we all remember now –
And airy voices, heard afar!
And three Magicians, and a Star!

Two thousand times of snow declare
That on the Christmas of the year
There is a singing in the air;
And all who listen for it hear
A fairy chime, a seraph strain,
Telling He is born again,
– That all we love is born again.

James Stephens (1882-1950)

SALUS MUNDI
The Safety of the World

I saw a stable, low and very bare,
    A little child in a manger.
The oxen knew Him, had Him in their care,
    To men He was a stranger.
The safety of the world was lying there,
    And the world's danger.

Mary Coleridge (1861-1907)

11

STABLE SONG

She lies, a stillness in the crumpled straw
Whilst he looks softly on the child, unsure,
And shadows waver by the stable door.

The oxen stir; a moth drifts through the bare
Outbuilding, silken Gabriel-winged, to where
She lies, a stillness in the crumpled straw.

A carpenter, his wife, both unaware
That kings and shepherds seek them from afar
And shadows waver by the stable door.

The child sleeps on. A drowse of asses snore;
He murmurs gently, raises eyes to her
Who lies, a stillness in the crumpled straw.

A cockerel crows, disturbed by sudden fear
As shepherds, dark upon the hill, appear
And shadows waver by the stable door.

The hush of birth is in the midnight air
And new life hides the distant smell of myrrh;
She lies, a stillness in the crumpled straw,
And shadows waver by the stable door.

Judith Nicholls

RAMONA AND THE
THREE WISE PERSONS

from Ramona and Her Father *by Beverly Cleary*

Ramona's big sister, Beezus, is to be Mary in the school Nativity play, so Ramona has volunteered to be a sheep, impulsively committing her overworked and hard-up mother to making her costume. Howie and Davy then offer to make up a flock of three.

Suddenly, a few days before Christmas when the Quimby family least expected it, the telephone rang for Ramona's father. He had a job! The morning after New Year's Day he was to report for training as a checker in a chain of supermarkets. The pay was good, he would have to work some evenings, and maybe someday he would get to manage a market!

After that telephone call Mr Quimby stopped reaching for cigarettes that were not there and began to whistle as he ran the vacuum cleaner and folded the clothes from the dryer. The worried frown disappeared from Mrs Quimby's forehead. Beezus looked even more calm and serene. Ramona, however, made a mistake. She told her mother about her tight shoes. Mrs Quimby then wasted a Saturday afternoon shopping for shoes when she could have been sewing on Ramona's costume. As a result, when they drove to church the night of the Christmas-carol programme, Ramona was the only unhappy member of the family.

Mr Quimby sang as he drove:

"There's a little wheel a-turning in my heart.

There's a little wheel a-turning in my heart."

Ramona loved that song because it made her think of Howie, who liked machines. Tonight, however, she was determined not to enjoy her father's singing.

Rain blew against the car, headlights shone on the pavement, the windscreen wipers *splip-splopped*. Mrs Quimby leaned back, tired but relaxed. Beezus smiled her gentle Virgin Mary smile that Ramona had found so annoying for the past three weeks.

Ramona sulked. Some place above those cold, wet clouds the very same star was shining that had guided the Three Wise Men to Bethlehem. On a night like this they never would have made it.

Mr Quimby sang on, "Oh, I feel like shouting in my heart..."

Ramona interrupted her father's song. "I don't care what anybody says," she burst out. "If I can't be a good sheep, I am not going to be a sheep at all." She yanked off the white terry-cloth head dress with pink-lined ears that she was wearing and stuffed it into the pocket of her car coat. She started to pull her father's rolled-down socks from her hands because they didn't really look like hooves, but then she decided they kept her hands warm. She squirmed on the lumpy terry-cloth tail sewn to the seat of her pyjamas. Ramona could not pretend that faded pyjamas printed with an army of pink rabbits, half of them upside down, made her look like a sheep, and Ramona was usually good at pretending.

Mrs Quimby's voice was tired. "Ramona, your tail and head-dress were all I could manage, and I had to stay up late last night to finish those. I simply don't have time for complicated sewing."

Ramona knew that. Her family had been telling her so for the past three weeks.

"A sheep should be woolly," said Ramona. "A sheep should not be printed with pink bunnies."

"You can be a sheep that has been shorn," said Mr Quimby, who was full of jokes now that he was going to work again. "Or how about a wolf in sheep's clothing?"

"You just want me to be miserable," said Ramona, not appreciating her father's humour and feeling that everyone in her family should be miserable because she was.

"She's worn out," said Mrs Quimby, as if Ramona could not hear. "It's so hard to wait for Christmas at her age."

Ramona raised her voice. "I am *not* worn out! You know sheep don't wear pyjamas."

"That's show biz," said Mr Quimby.

"Daddy!" Beezus-Mary was shocked. "It's church!"

"And don't forget, Ramona," said Mr Quimby, "as my grandmother would have said, 'Those pink bunnies will never be noticed from a trotting horse.'"

Ramona disliked her father's grandmother even more. Besides, nobody rode trotting horses in church.

The sight of light shining through the stained-glass window of the big stone church diverted Ramona for a moment. The window looked beautiful, as if it were made of jewels.

Mr Quimby backed the car into a parking space. "Ho-ho-ho!" he said, as he turned off the ignition. "'Tis the season to be jolly."

Jolly was the last thing Ramona was going to be. Leaving the car, she stooped down inside her car coat to hide as many rabbits as possible. Black branches clawed at the sky, and the wind was raw.

"Stand up straight," said Ramona's heartless father.

"I'll get wet," said Ramona. "I might catch cold, and then you'd be sorry."

"Run between the drops," said Mr Quimby.

"They're too close together," answered Ramona.

"Oh, you two," said Mrs Quimby with a tired little laugh, as she backed out of the car and tried to open her umbrella at the same time.

"I will not be in it." Ramona defied her family once and for all. "They can give the programme without me."

Her father's answer was a surprise. "Suit yourself," he said. "You're not

15

going to spoil our evening."

Mrs Quimby gave the seat of Ramona's pyjamas an affectionate pat. "Run along, little lamb, wagging your tail behind you."

Ramona walked stiff-legged so that her tail would not wag.

At the church door the family parted, the girls going downstairs to the Sunday-school room, which was a confusion of chattering children piling coats and raincoats on chairs. Ramona found a corner behind the Christmas tree, where Santa would pass out candy canes after the programme. She sat down on the floor with her car coat over her bent knees.

Through the branches Ramona watched carollers putting on their white robes. Girls were tying tinsel around one another's heads while Mrs Russo searched out boys and tied tinsel around their heads, too. "It's all right for boys to wear tinsel," Mrs Russo assured them. Some looked as if they were not certain they believed her.

One boy climbed on a chair. "I'm an angel. Watch me fly," he announced and jumped off, flapping the wide sleeves of his choir robe. All the carollers turned into flapping angels.

Nobody noticed Ramona. Everyone was having too much fun. Shepherds found their cloaks, which were made from old cotton bedspreads. Beezus's friend, Henry Huggins, arrived and put on the dark robe he was to wear in the part of Joseph.

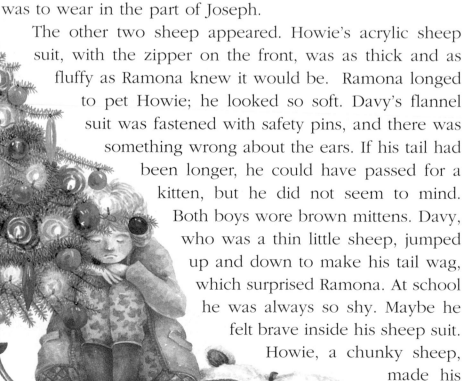

The other two sheep appeared. Howie's acrylic sheep suit, with the zipper on the front, was as thick and as fluffy as Ramona knew it would be. Ramona longed to pet Howie; he looked so soft. Davy's flannel suit was fastened with safety pins, and there was something wrong about the ears. If his tail had been longer, he could have passed for a kitten, but he did not seem to mind. Both boys wore brown mittens. Davy, who was a thin little sheep, jumped up and down to make his tail wag, which surprised Ramona. At school he was always so shy. Maybe he felt brave inside his sheep suit. Howie, a chunky sheep, made his tail wag, too. My ears are as good as theirs, Ramona told herself. The floor felt cold through the seat of her thin pyjamas.

"Look at the little lambs!" cried an angel. "Aren't they darling?"

"Ba-a, ba-a!" bleated Davy and Howie.

Ramona longed to be there with them, jumping and ba-a-ing and wagging her tail, too. Maybe the faded rabbits didn't show as much as she had thought. She sat hunched and miserable. She had told her father she would *not* be a sheep, and she couldn't back down now. She hoped God was too busy to notice her, and then she changed her mind. Please, God, prayed Ramona, in case He wasn't too busy to listen to a miserable little sheep, I don't really mean to be horrid. It just works out that way. She was frightened, she discovered, for when the programme began, she would be left alone in the church basement. The lights might even be turned out, a scary thought, for the big stone church filled Ramona with awe, and she did not want to be left alone in the dark with her awe. Please, God, prayed Ramona, get me out of this mess.

Beezus, in a long blue robe with a white scarf over her head and carrying a baby's blanket and a big flashlight, found her little sister. "Come out, Ramona," she coaxed. "Nobody will notice your costume. You know Mother would have made you a whole sheep suit if she had time. Be a good sport. Please."

Ramona shook her head and blinked to keep tears from falling. "I told Daddy I wouldn't be in the programme, and I won't."

"Well, OK, if that's the way you feel," said Beezus, forgetting to act like Mary. She left her little sister to her misery.

Ramona sniffed and wiped her eyes on her hoof. Why didn't some grown-up come along and *make* her join the other sheep? No grown-up came. No one seemed to remember there were supposed to be three sheep, not even Howie, who played with her almost every day.

Ramona's eye caught the reflection of her face distorted in a green Christmas ornament. She was shocked to see her nose look huge, her mouth and red-rimmed eyes tiny. I can't really look like that, thought Ramona in despair. I'm really a nice person. It's just that nobody understands.

Ramona mopped her eyes on her hoof again, and as she did she noticed three big girls, so tall they were probably in the eighth grade, putting on robes made from better bedspreads than the shepherd's robes.

17

That's funny, she thought. Nothing she had learned in Sunday school told her anything about girls in long robes in the Nativity scene. Could they be Jesus's aunts?

One of the girls began to dab tan cream from a little jar on her face and to smear it around while another girl held up a pocket mirror. The third girl, holding her own mirror, used an eyebrow pencil to give herself heavy brows.

Make-up, thought Ramona with interest, wishing she could wear it. The girls took turns darkening their faces and brows. They looked like different people. Ramona got to her knees and peered over the lower branches of the Christmas tree for a better view.

One of the girls noticed her. "Hi, there," she said. "Why are you hiding back there?"

"Because," was Ramona's all-purpose answer. "Are you Jesus's aunts?" she asked.

The girls found the question funny. "No," answered one. "We're the Three Wise Persons."

Ramona was puzzled. "I thought they were supposed to be wise *men*," she said.

"The boys backed out at the last minute," explained the girl with the blackest eyebrows. "Mrs Russo said women can be wise too, so tonight we are the Three Wise Persons."

This idea seemed like a good one to Ramona, who wished she were big enough to be a wise person hiding behind make-up so nobody would know who she was.

"Are you supposed to be in the programme?" asked one of the girls.

"I was supposed to be a sheep, but I changed my mind," said Ramona, changing it back again. She pulled out her sheep headdress and put it on.

"Isn't that adorable?" said one of the wise persons.

Ramona was surprised. She had never been called adorable before. Bright, lively, yes; adorable, no. She smiled and felt more lovable. Maybe pink-lined ears helped.

"Why don't you want to be a sheep?" asked a wise person.

Ramona had an inspiration. "Because I don't have any make-up."

"Make-up on a *sheep*!" exclaimed a wise person and giggled.

Ramona persisted. "Sheep have black noses," she hinted. "Maybe I could have a black nose."

The girls looked at one another. "Don't tell my mother," said one, "but I have some mascara. We could make her nose black."

"Please!" begged Ramona, getting to her feet and coming out from behind the Christmas tree.

The owner of the mascara fumbled in her shoulder bag, which was hanging on a chair, and brought out a tiny box. "Let's go in the kitchen where there's a sink," she said, and when Ramona followed her, she moistened an elf-sized brush, which she rubbed on the mascara in the box. Then she began to brush it on to Ramona's nose. It tickled, but Ramona held still. "It feels like brushing my teeth only on my nose," she remarked. The wise person stood back to look at her work and then applied another coat of mascara to Ramona's nose. "There," she said at last. "Now you look like a real sheep."

Ramona felt like a real sheep. "Ba-a-a," she bleated, a sheep's way of saying thank you. Ramona felt so much better, she could almost pretend she was woolly. She peeled off her coat and found that the faded pink rabbits really didn't show much in the dim light. She pranced off among the angels, who had been handed flashlights, which they were supposed to hold like candles. Instead they were shining them into their mouths to show one another how weird they looked with light showing through their cheeks. The other two sheep stopped jumping when they saw her.

"You don't look like Ramona," said Howie.

"Ba-a-a. I'm not Ramona. I'm a sheep." The boys did not say one word about Ramona's pyjamas. They wanted black noses too, and when Ramona told them where she got hers, they ran off to find the wise persons. When they returned, they no longer looked like Howie and Davy in sheep suits. They looked like strangers in sheep suits. So I must really look like somebody else, thought Ramona with increasing happiness. Now she could be in the programme, and her parents wouldn't know because they wouldn't recognise her.

"B-a-a!" bleated three prancing, black-nosed sheep. "B-a-a, b-a-a."

Mrs Russo clapped her hands. "Quiet, everybody!" she ordered. "All right, Mary and Joseph, up by the front stairs. Shepherds and sheep next and then wise persons. Angels line up by the back stairs."

The three sheep pranced over to the shepherds, one of whom said, "Look what we get to herd," and nudged Ramona with his crook.

"You cut that out," said Ramona.

"Quietly, everyone," said Mrs Russo.

Ramona's heart began to pound as if something exciting were about to happen. Up the stairs she tiptoed and through the arched door. The only light came from candelabra on either side of the chancel and from a street light shining through a stained-glass window. Ramona had never seen the church look so beautiful or so mysterious.

Beezus sat down on a low stool in the centre of the chancel and arranged the baby's blanket around the flashlight. Henry stood behind her. The sheep got down on their hands and knees in front of the shepherds, and the Three Wise Persons stood off to one side, holding bath-salts jars that looked as if they really could hold frankincense and myrrh. An electric star suspended above the organ began to shine. Beezus turned on the big flashlight inside the baby's blanket and light shone up on her face, making her look like a picture of Mary on a Christmas card. From the rear door a wobbly procession of kindergarten angels, holding their small flashlights like candles, led the way, glimmering, two by two.

"Ah..." breathed the congregation.

"Hark, the herald angels sing," the advancing angels carolled. They looked nothing like the jumping, flapping mob with flashlights shining through their cheeks that Ramona had watched downstairs. They looked good and serious and... holy.

A shivery feeling ran down Ramona's backbone, as if magic were taking place. She looked up at Beezus, smiling tenderly down at the flashlight, and it seemed as if Baby Jesus really could be inside the blanket. Why, thought Ramona with a feeling of shock, Beezus looks nice. Kind and – sort of pretty. Ramona had never thought of her sister as anything but – well, a plain old big sister, who got to do everything first. Ramona was suddenly proud of Beezus. Maybe they did fight a lot when Beezus wasn't going around acting like Mary, but Beezus was never really mean.

As the carollers bore more light into the church, Ramona found her parents in the second row. They were smiling gently, proud of Beezus, too. This gave Ramona an aching feeling inside. They would not know her in her make-up. Maybe they would think she was some other sheep. She wanted to be their sheep. She wanted them to be proud of her, too.

Ramona saw her father look away from Beezus and look directly at her. Did he recognise her? Yes, he did. Mr Quimby winked. Ramona was shocked. Winking in church! How could her father do such a thing? He winked again and this time held up his thumb and forefinger in a circle. Ramona understood. Her father was telling her he was proud of her, too.

"Joy to the newborn King!" sang the angels, as they mounted the steps on either side of the chancel.

Ramona was filled with joy. Christmas was the most beautiful, magic time of the whole year. Her parents loved her, and she loved them, and Beezus, too. At home there was a Christmas tree and under it, presents, fewer than at past Christmases, but presents all the same. Ramona could not contain her feelings. "B-a-a," she bleated joyfully.

She felt the nudge of a shepherd's crook on the seat of her pyjamas and heard her shepherd whisper through clenched teeth, "You be quiet!" Ramona did not bleat again. She wiggled her seat to make her tail wag.

22

MINSTREL'S SONG

I've just had an astounding dream as I lay in the straw.
I dreamed a star fell on to the straw beside me
And lay blazing. Then when I looked up
I saw a bull come flying through a sky of fire
And on its shoulders a huge silver woman
Holding the moon. And afterwards there came
A donkey flying through that same burning heaven
And on its shoulders a colossal man
Holding the sun. Suddenly I awoke
And saw a bull and a donkey kneeling in the straw,
And the great moving shadows of a man and a woman –
I say they were a man and a woman but
I dare not say what I think they were. I did not dare to look.
I ran out here into the freezing world
Because I dared not look. Inside that shed.

A star is coming this way along the road.
If I were not standing upright, this would be a dream.
A star the shape of a sword of fire, point-downward,
Is floating along the road. And now it rises.
It is shaking fire on to the roofs and the gardens.
And now it rises above the animal shed
Where I slept till the dream woke me. And now
The star is standing over the animal shed.

Ted Hughes

THE INNKEEPER'S WIFE

I love this byre. Shadows are kindly here.
The light is flecked with travelling stars of dust.
So quiet it seems after thé inn-clamour,
Scraping of fiddles and the stamping feet.
Only the cows, each in her patient box,
Turn their slow eyes, as we and the sunlight enter,
Their slowly rhythmic mouths. "That is the stall,
Carpenter. You see it's too far gone
For patching or repatching. My husband made it,
And he's been gone these dozen years and more..."
Strange how this lifeless thing, degraded wood
Split from the tree and nailed and crucified
To make a wal!, outlives the mastering hand
That struck it down, the warm firm hand
That touched my body with its wandering love.
"No, let the fire take them. Strip every board
And make a new beginning. Too many memories lurk
Like worms in this old wood. That piece you're holding –
That patch of grain with the giant's thumbprint –
I stared at it a full hour when he died:
Its grooves are down my mind. And that board there
Baring its knot-hole like a missing jig-saw –
I remember another hand along its rim.
No, not my husband's, and why I should remember
I cannot say. It was a night in winter.
Our house was full, tight-packed as salted herrings –
So full, they said, we had to hold our breaths
To close the door and shut the night-air out!
And then two travellers came. They stood outside
Across the threshold, half in the ring of light
And half beyond it. I would have let them in
Despite the crowding – the woman was past her time –
But I'd no mind to argue with my husband,

The flagon in my hand and half the inn
Still clamouring for wine. But when trade slackened,
And all our guests had sung themselves to bed
Or told the floor their troubles, I came out here
Where he had lodged them. The man was standing
As you are now, his hand smoothing that board.–
He was a carpenter, I heard them say.
She rested on the straw, and on her arm
A child was lying. None of your creased-faced brats
Squalling their lungs out. Just lying there
As calm as a new-dropped calf – his eyes wide open,
And gazing round as if the world he saw
In the chaff-strewn light of the stable lantern
Was something beautiful and new and strange.
Ah well, he'll have learnt different now, I reckon,
Wherever he is. And why I should recall
A scene like that, when times I would remember
Have passed beyond reliving, I cannot think.
It's a trick you're served by old possessions:
They have their memories too – too many memories.
Well, I must go in. There are meals to serve.
Join us there, Carpenter, when you've had enough
Of cattle-company. The world is a sad place,
But wine and music blunt the truth of it."

Clive Sansom

THE OXEN

Christmas Eve, and twelve of the clock.
"Now they are all on their knees,"
An elder said, as we sat in a flock,
By the embers in fireside ease.

We pictured the meek mild creatures, where
They dwelt in their strawy pen,
Nor did it occur to one of us there
To doubt they were kneeling then.

So fair a fancy few would weave
In these years! Yet, I feel
If someone said, on Christmas Eve,
"Come; see the oxen kneel

"In the lonely barton by yonder coomb,
Our childhood used to know,"
I should go with him in the gloom,
Hoping it might be so.

Thomas Hardy (1840-1928)

WHAT THE DONKEY SAW

No room in the inn, of course,
And not that much in the stable,
What with the shepherds, Magi, Mary,
Joseph, the heavenly host –
Not to mention the baby
Using our manger as a cot.
You couldn't have squeezed another cherub in
For love or money.

Still, in spite of the overcrowding,
I did my best to make them feel wanted.
I could see the baby and I
Would be going places together.

U. A. Fanthorpe

MICE IN THE HAY

out of the lamplight
  whispering worshipping
the mice in the hay

timid eyes pearl-bright
  whispering worshipping
whisking quick and away

they were there that night
  whispering worshipping
smaller than snowflakes are

quietly made their way
  whispering worshipping
close to the manger

yes, they were afraid
  whispering worshipping
as the journey was made

from a dark corner
  whispering worshipping
scuttling together

But He smiled to see them
  whispering worshipping
there in the lamplight

stretched out His hand to them
  they saw the baby King
hurried back out of sight
  whispering worshipping

Leslie Norris

HOW FAR TO BETHLEHEM?

How far is it to Bethlehem?
Not very far.
Shall we find the stable-room
Lit by a star?

Can we see the little child,
Is He within?
If we lift the wooden latch
May we go in?

May we stroke the creatures there,
Ox, ass and sheep?
May we peep like them and see
Jesus asleep?

If we touch His tiny hand
Will He awake?
Will He know we've come so far
Just for His sake?

Great kings have precious gifts,
And we have naught;
Little smiles and little tears
Are all we brought.

For all weary children
Mary must weep.
Here on His bed of straw
Sleep, children, sleep.

God in His mother's arm,
Babes in the byre
Sleep as they sleep who find
Their heart's desire.

Frances Chesterton

THE STORY OF THE STAR

1

One, two, three camels.

One, two, three Wise Men.

Pad, pad, pad, went the camels' feet over the sand.

Clang-a-ling-ling-ling went the bells on the harness.

Three Wise Men rode swiftly over the sand. It was night. They kept their eyes on a big star. The big star sparkled and shone.

2

One, two, three camels.

One, two, three Wise Men.

The camels' feet did not go pad, pad, pad.

The camels were resting.

The bells on the harness did not go clang-a-ling-ling-ling. The Wise Men were resting. The sun was hot.

Then it was night again. One by one the stars came out. The big star sparkled and shone.

Pad, pad, pad, went the camels' feet over the sand.

Clang-a-ling-ling-ling went the bells on the harness.

3

Three Wise Men rode swiftly over the sand.

They came to the gates of a city. The people came out to meet them.

"Where is the Baby who is born to be the King?" asked the Wise Men. "We have seen His star in the sky. We have come to bring Him gifts."

The people shook their heads.

The three Wise Men rode up and down the streets.

"Where is the Baby who is born to be the King?" asked the Wise Men. "We have seen His star in the sky. We have come to bring Him gifts."

The people shook their heads.

Then it was night again. One by one the stars came out. The big star sparkled and shone. The Wise Men were happy. Now they could find the Baby.

Pad, pad, pad, went the camels' feet.

Clang-a-ling-ling-ling went the bells on the harness.

4

The big star sparkled and shone. It seemed to stand over a little house.

The camels kneeled. The Wise Men got off. They went into the little house. They found Jesus and His mother.

The Wise Men went out to the camels. They took their gifts from the camels' backs. They bowed low before the Baby Jesus. They gave Him their gifts.

Jessie Eleanor Moore

AT NINE OF THE NIGHT
I OPENED MY DOOR

At nine of the night I opened my door
That stands midway between moor and moor,
And all around me, silver-bright,
I saw that the world had turned to white.

Thick was the snow on field and hedge
And vanished was the river-sedge,
Where winter skilfully had wound
A shining scarf without a sound.

And as I stood and gazed my fill
A stable-boy came down the hill.
With every step I saw him take
Flew at his heel a puff of flake.

His brow was whiter than the hoar,
A beard of freshest snow he wore,
And round about him, snowflake starred,
A red horse-blanket from the yard.

In a red cloak I saw him go,
His back was bent, his step was slow,
And as he laboured through the cold
He seemed a hundred winters old.

I stood and watched the snowy head,
The whiskers white, the cloak of red.
"A Merry Christmas!" I heard him cry.
"The same to you, old friend," said I.

Charles Causley

BAH! HUMBUG!

from A Christmas Carol
by Charles Dickens (1812-1870)

Once upon a time – of all the good days in the year, on Christmas Eve – old Scrooge sat busy in his counting-house. It was cold, bleak, biting weather; foggy withal; and he could hear the people in the court outside go wheezing up and down, beating their hands upon their breasts, and stamping their feet upon the pavement stones to warm them. The City clocks had only just gone three, but it was quite dark already – it had not been light all day – and candles were flaring in the windows of the neighbouring offices, like ruddy smears upon the palpable brown air. The fog came pouring in at every chink and key-hole, and was so dense without, that, although the court was of the narrowest, the houses opposite were mere phantoms. To see the dingy cloud come drooping down, obscuring everything, one might have thought that nature lived hard by, and was brewing on a large scale.

The door of Scrooge's counting-house was open, that he might keep his eye upon his clerk, who in a dismal little cell beyond, a sort of tank, was copying letters. Scrooge had a very small fire, but the clerk's fire was so very much smaller that it looked like one coal.

But he couldn't replenish it, for Scrooge kept the coal-box in his own room; and so surely as the clerk came in with the shovel, the master predicted that it would be necessary for them to part. Wherefore the clerk put on his white comforter, and tried to warm himself at the candle; in which effort, not being a man of strong imagination, he failed.

"A merry Christmas, uncle! God save you!" cried a cheerful voice. It was the voice of Scrooge's nephew, who came upon him so quickly that this was the first intimation he had of his approach.

"Bah!" said Scrooge. "Humbug!"

He had so heated himself with rapid walking in the fog and frost, this nephew of Scrooge's, that he was all in a glow; his face was ruddy and handsome; his eyes sparkled, and his breath smoked again.

"Christmas a humbug, uncle!" said Scrooge's nephew. "You don't mean that, I am sure?"

"I do," said Scrooge. "Merry Christmas! What right have you to be merry? What reason have you to be merry? You're poor enough."

"Come, then," returned the nephew gaily. "What right have you to be dismal? What reason have you to be morose? You're rich enough."

Scrooge, having no better answer ready on the spur of the moment, said, "Bah!" again; and followed it up with "Humbug!"

"Don't be cross, uncle!" said the nephew.

"What else can I be," returned the uncle, "when I live in such a world of fools as this? Merry Christmas! Out upon merry Christmas! What's Christmas-time to you but a time for paying bills without money; a time for finding yourself a year older, and not an hour richer; a time for balancing your books, and having every item in 'em through a round dozen of months presented dead against you? If I could work my will," said Scrooge indignantly, "every idiot who goes about with 'Merry Christmas' on his lips should be boiled with his own pudding, and buried with a stake of holly through his heart. He should!"

"Uncle!" pleaded the nephew.

"Nephew!" returned the uncle sternly, "keep Christmas in your own way, and let me keep it in mine."

"Keep it!" repeated Scrooge's nephew. "But you don't keep it."

"Let me leave it alone, then," said Scrooge. "Much good may it do you! Much good it has ever done you!"

"There are many things from which I might have derived good, by which I have not profited, I dare say," returned the nephew; "Christmas among the rest. But I am sure I have always thought of Christmas-time, when it has come round – apart from the veneration due to its sacred name and origin, if anything belonging to it can be apart from that – as a good time; a kind, forgiving, charitable, pleasant time; the only time I know of, in the long calendar of the year, when men and women seem by one consent to open their shut-up hearts freely, and to think of people below them as if they really were fellow-passengers to the grave, and not another race of creatures bound on other journeys. And therefore, uncle, though it has never put a scrap of gold or silver in my pocket, I believe that it *has* done me good and *will* do me good; and I say, God bless it!"

The clerk in the tank involuntarily applauded. Becoming immediately sensible of the impropriety, he poked the fire, and extinguished the last frail spark for ever.

"Let me hear another sound from *you*," said Scrooge, "and you'll keep your Christmas by losing your situation! You're quite a powerful speaker, sir," he added, turning to his nephew. "I wonder you don't go into Parliament."

"Don't be angry, uncle. Come! Dine with us tomorrow."

Scrooge said that he would see him – Yes, indeed he did. He went the whole length of the expression, and said that he would see him in that extremity first.

"But why?" cried Scrooge's nephew. "Why?"

"Why did you get married?" said Scrooge.

"Because I fell in love."

"Because you fell in love!" growled Scrooge, as if that were the only one thing in the world more ridiculous than a merry Christmas. "Good afternoon!"

"Nay, uncle, but you never came to see me before that happened. Why give it as a reason for not coming now?"

"Good afternoon," said Scrooge.

"I want nothing from you; I ask nothing of you; why cannot we be friends?"

"Good afternoon!" said Scrooge.

"I am sorry, with all my heart, to find you so resolute. We have never had any quarrel to which I have been a party. But I have made the trial in homage to Christmas, and I'll keep my Christmas humour to the last. So A Merry Christmas, uncle!"

"Good afternoon," said Scrooge.

"And A Happy New Year!"

"Good afternoon!" said Scrooge.

His nephew left the room without an angry word, notwithstanding. He stopped at the outer door to bestow the greetings of the season on the clerk, who, cold as he was, was warmer than Scrooge; for he returned them cordially.

"There's another fellow," muttered Scrooge, who overheard him: "my clerk, with fifteen shillings a week, and a wife and family, talking about a merry Christmas. I'll retire to Bedlam."

THE
MIDWINTER FEAST

GOOD WILL TO MEN – CHRISTMAS GREETINGS IN SIX LANGUAGES

At Christmas, when old friends are meeting,
We give that long-loved joyous greeting –
    "Merry Christmas!"

While hanging sheaves for winter birds
Friends in Norway call the words,
    "God Jul!"

With wooden shoes ranged on the hearth,
Dutch celebrators cry their mirth,
    "Vrolyk Kerstfeest!"

In France, that land of courtesy,
Our welcome to our guests would be,
    "Joyeux Noël!"

Enshrining Christmas in her art,
Italy cries from a full heart,
    "Buon Natale!"

When in the land of Christmas trees,
Old Germany, use words like these –
    "Fröhliche Weihnachten!"

Though each land names a different name,
Good will rings through each wish the same –
    "Merry Christmas!"

Dorothy Brown Thompson

OUR JOYFULL'ST FEAST

So, now is come our joyfull'st feast;
Let every man be jolly.
Each room with ivy-leaves is dressed,
And every post with holly.
　　Though some churls at our mirth repine,
　　Round your foreheads garlands twine,
　　Drown sorrow in a cup of wine,
And let us all be merry.

Now, all our neighbours' chimneys smoke,
And Christmas blocks are burning;
Their ovens, they with baked meats choke,
And all their spits are turning.
　　Without the door let sorrow lie,
　　And if for cold it hap to die,
　　We'll bury it in a Christmas pie,
And evermore be merry.

Then wherefore in these merry days,
Should we I pray, be duller?
No; let us sing some roundelays
To make our mirth the fuller.
　　And, whilst thus inspired we sing,
　　Let all the streets with echoes ring:
　　Woods, and hills, and everything,
Bear witness we are merry.

George Wither
A Christmas Carol, from Faire-Virtue, 1622

WASSAILING SONG

Wisselton, wasselton, who lives here?
We've come to taste your Christmas beer.
Up the kitchen and down the hall,
Holly, ivy, and mistletoe;
A peck of apples will serve us all,
Give us some apples and let us go.

Up with your stocking, on with your shoe,
If you haven't got any apples, money will do.
My carol's done, and I must be gone,
No longer can I stay here.
God bless you all, great and small,
And send you a happy new year.

Traditional

CHRISTMAS

Christmas is come, and every hearth
Makes room to give him welcome now.
E'en want will dry its tears in mirth
And crown him wi' a holly bough,
Though tramping 'neath a winter's sky
O'er snow track paths and rimey stiles.
The housewife sets her spinning by,
And bids him welcome wi' her smiles.

The shepherd, now no more afraid
Since custom doth the chance bestow,
Starts up to kiss the giggling maid
Beneath the branch of mistletoe
That 'neath each cottage beam is seen,
Wi' pearl-like berries shining gay,
The shadow still of what hath been
Which fashion yearly fades away.

And singers too, a merry throng,
At early morn wi' simple skill
Yet imitate the angels' song,
And chant their Christmas ditty still.
And, 'mid the storm that dies and swells
In fits, in hummings softly steals
The music of the village bells
Ringing round their merry peals.

And when it's passed, a merry crew
Bedecked in masks and ribbons gay
The "Morris dance" their sports renew,
And act their winter evening play:
The clown-turned-kings, for penny praise,
Storm wi' the actors' strut and swell,
And harlequin, a laugh to raise,
Wears his hump-back and tinkling bell.

And oft for pence and spicy ale,
Wi' winter nosegays pinned before,
The wassail singer tells her tale,
And drawls her Christmas carols o'er.
The 'prentice boy, wi' ruddy face
And rime-bepowdered dancing locks,
From door to door wi' happy pace
Runs round to claim his "Christmas box".

John Clare (1793-1864)

41

BIRD SURPRISE

Take a large olive, stone it and then stuff it with a paste made of anchovy, capers and oil.

Put the olive inside a trussed and boned bec-figue.

Put the bec-figue inside a fat ortolan.

Put the ortolan inside a boned lark.

Put the stuffed lark inside a boned thrush.

Put the thrush inside a fat quail.

Put the quail, wrapped in vine leaves, inside a boned lapwing.

Put the lapwing inside a boned golden plover.

Put the plover inside a fat, boned, red-legged partridge.

Put the partridge inside a young, boned, and well-hung woodcock.

Put the woodcock, rolled in bread-crumbs, inside a boned teal.

Put the teal inside a boned guinea-fowl.

Put the guinea-fowl, well-larded, inside a young and boned tame duck.

Put the duck inside a boned and fat fowl.

Put the fowl inside a well-hung pheasant.

Put the pheasant inside a boned and fat wild goose.

Put the goose inside a fine turkey.

Put the turkey inside a boned bustard.

Having arranged your roast after this fashion, place it in a large saucepan with onions stuffed with cloves, carrots, small squares of ham, celery, mignonette, several strips of bacon well-seasoned, pepper, salt, spice, coriander seeds and two cloves of garlic.

Seal the saucepan hermetically by closing it with pastry. Then put it for ten hours over a gentle fire, and arrange it so that the heat can penetrate evenly. An oven moderately heated will suit better than the hearth.

Before serving, remove the pastry, put the roast on a hot dish after having removed the grease – if there is any – and serve.

Traditional, c. 1814

MISTLETOE

Mistletoe new,
Mistletoe old,
Cut it down
With a knife of gold.

Mistletoe green,
Mistletoe milk,
Let it fall
On a scarf of silk.

Mistletoe from
The Christmas oak,
Keep my house
From lightning stroke.

Guard from thunder
My roof-tree
And any evil
That there be.

Charles Causley

MR POOTER PROVOKES A DISMAYING EXPERIMENT

from The Diary of a Nobody
by George (1847-1912) and Weedon (1853-1919) Grossmith

Christmas Day

We caught the 10.20 train at Paddington, and spent a pleasant day at Carrie's mother's. The country was quite nice and pleasant, although the roads were sloppy. We dined in the middle of the day, just ten of us, and talked over old times. If everybody had a nice *un*interfering mother-in-law, such as I have, what a deal of happiness there would be in the world. Being all in good spirits, I proposed her health; and I made, I think, a very good speech.

I concluded, rather neatly, by saying: "On an occasion like this – whether relatives, friends, or acquaintances – we are all inspired with good feelings towards each other. We are of one mind, and think only of love and friendship. Those who have quarrelled with absent friends should kiss and make it up. Those who happily have *not* fallen out, can kiss all the same."

I saw the tears in the eyes of both Carrie and her mother, and must say I felt very flattered by the compliment. That dear old Reverend John Panzy Smith, who married us, made a most cheerful and amusing speech, and said he should act on my suggestion respecting the kissing. He then walked round the table and kissed all the ladies, including Carrie. Of course one did not object to this; but I was more than staggered when a young fellow named Moss, who was a stranger to me, and who had scarcely spoken a word through dinner, jumped up suddenly with a sprig of mistletoe, and exclaimed: "Hulloh! I don't see why I shouldn't be on in this scene." Before one could realise what he was about to do, he kissed Carrie and the rest of the ladies.

Fortunately the matter was treated as a joke, and we all laughed; but it was a dangerous experiment, and I felt very uneasy for a moment as to the result. I subsequently referred to the matter to Carrie, but she said: "Oh, he's not much more than a boy." I said that he had a very large moustache for a boy. Carrie replied: "I didn't say he was not a nice boy."

THE BEST GIFT

At Christmas most of us have fun:
Some say, because God sent his Son.
But it's a time I wouldn't miss
For all those chances of a kiss
From Mum, or Dad, Grandad or Gran,
Your girl or boy, your wife or man.
Indeed, that pleasure I derive
From Christmas 1985
(Trafalgar Square, a girl, a tree)
My Venetian lady got from me –
Being, I was surprised to know,
The first time she'd used mistletoe.
The Wise Men's gifts were splendid things,
But it is kisses makes us Kings.

Todd Hamilton

CHRISTMAS DAY

Small girls on trikes
Bigger on bikes
Collars on tykes

Looking like cads
Patterned in plaids
Scarf-wearing dads

Chewing a choc
Mum in a frock
Watches the clock

Knocking in pans
Fetching of grans
Gathering of clans

Hissing from tins
Sherries and gins
Upping of chins

Corks making pops
"Just a few drops"
Watering of chops

All this odd joy
Tears at a broken toy
Just for the birth long ago of a boy

Roy Fuller (1912-1991)

I REMEMBER YULE

I guess I am just an old fogey.
I guess I am headed for the last round-up, so come along little dogey.
I can remember when winter was wintery and summer was estival;
I can even remember when Christmas was a family festival.
Yes, I can remember when Christmas was an occasion for fireside
        rejoicing and general goodwill,
And now it is just the day that it's only X shopping days until.
I can remember when we knew Christmas was coming without being
        reminded by the sponsor
And the annoncer.
What, five times a week at 8.15 p.m., do the herald angels sing?
That a small deposit now will buy you an option on a genuine
        diamond ring.
What is the message we receive with Good King Wenceslaus?
That if we rush to the corner of Ninth and Main we can get that
        pink mink housecoat very inexpenceslaus.
I know what came upon the midnight clear to our backward parents,
        but what comes to us?
A choir imploring us to Come all ye faithful and steal a 1939
        convertible at psychoneurotic prices from Grinning Gus.
Christmas is a sitting duck for sponsors, it's so commercial,
And yet so noncontroversial.
Well, you reverent sponsors redolent of frankincense and myrrh, come
        smear me with bear-grease and call me an un-American hellion,
This is my declaration of independence and rebellion.
This year I'm going to disconnect everything electrical in the house
        and spend the Christmas season like Tiny Tim and Mr Pickwick;
You make me sickwick.

Ogden Nash (1902-1971)

GHOSTS FROM A CHRISTMAS PAST

Cyclamens

These were the Christmas plants
For my several blossomless aunts.

Sad they looked, their petalled faces
Pale, as they journeyed to the wrong places

With me beside them on the back seat
And Dad driving us from street to street.

He'd wait in the car while I took them in,
Was thanked, kissed, and came out again

Until all were delivered, a good job done
By the seasonal firm of Father and Son,

But we left behind us the treacherous chill
Of a slow death on each maiden window-sill.

The Torch

Bringing light
Beneath our stairs
Dad blessed the boxes
Unawares.

A kindly, quick
Redemptive ray
Lit last year's Christmas
Stacked away.

I use it now
And raise a ghost
Tangled with tinsel's
Bitter frost

Who hands it over
To my son
Then leaves the world
He'll shine it on.

The Walk

Over the hills, but never far away,
He took us for a run on Boxing Day.

After the oxtail soup, the ham, the tongue,
We put on coats, thick socks and wellingtons

And went, with ritual grindings of the gear,
Exactly where we'd gone this time last year.

We took the scenic walk exactly too,
My mother rhapsodising on the view,

My father silent, gazing straight ahead
As if already somewhere else instead.

Then, on the dot, we'd take the same route back
In time for fancy cakes and Uncle Mac.

John Mole

49

THE MOOMINS
DEAL WITH CHRISTMAS

A Story by Tove Jansson

Moomins, sticklers for tradition, always sleep from November to April, grouped round the biggest porcelain stove in the house, and with everything they might need laid ready for spring. They live in Moominvalley with their many "curious but likeable" friends – such as the Hemulen who, like all Hemulens, has had a strict upbringing and wears an awful lot of clothes (no one knows why).

I

The Hemulen scratched and scratched in the snow. He was wearing yellow woollen gloves and, of course, before long they became very wet and uncomfortable. So he took them off and carefully placed them on the chimney stack, sighed, and went on scratching; then at last he uncovered the attic window.

"Ah, here it is," said the Hemulen. "And down there they're lying asleep. Sleeping and sleeping and sleeping. And others have to work themselves to death, all because it's nearly Christmas. By my tail!"

He stepped on to the skylight, trying to remember if it opened inwards or outwards. He stamped on it, and it immediately opened inwards. Down the Hemulen tumbled into the snow and darkness, falling on to all those things which the Moomin family had stowed in the attic – to use later.

By now, he was very much annoyed, and besides, he could not quite remember where he had put the yellow woollen gloves that he was so fond of. So he stamped down the stairs and shouted in an angry voice:

"It's going to be Christmas. I'm vexed with you, and your sleeping, and it's going to be Christmas any minute now."

Down below all the Moomin family lay in their snug winter retreat. They had slept for several months and intended to go on sleeping until spring – the Moomins love to forget about winter in this way. They slept as softly and comfortably as on a long warm summer afternoon. Now sudden anxiety, or perhaps it was cold air, broke in upon Moomintroll's dreams. Someone was pulling the quilt off him and was shouting that it was vexed with him, and that it was going to be Christmas.

"Is it spring already?" murmured Moomintroll.

"Spring?" exclaimed the Hemulen irritably. "It's Christmas, don't you know? – Christmas. And I haven't got anything, and nothing's arranged; and then in the middle of it all, they send me to dig you out. I've lost my yellow gloves, I expect, and everyone's running round in circles, and nothing's ready..."

And the Hemulen stamped up the stairs again and climbed out of the attic skylight.

"Mamma! Wake up!" called Moomintroll, frightened. "Something awful's happened. They call it Christmas."

"What do you mean?" said Moominmamma and put out her nose.

"I don't know really," said her son. "But nothing's arranged, and someone's lost and everyone's running round in circles. Perhaps it's the water rising again."

He shook the Snork Maiden gently and whispered:

"Don't be frightened, but something awful's happened."

"Calm!" said Moominpappa. "Calm above all!"

And he went to wind up the clock which had read a quarter to nine since sometime in October.

They followed the Hemulen's wet footsteps up to the attic and stepped out on the roof of Moominhouse. The sky was beautifully blue, so there was evidently no question of another volcanic eruption.

But the entire valley was covered in wet cotton wool – the hills, the trees,

the river and the whole house. And it was cold – colder even than in April.

"Is this what they call Christmas?" asked Moominmamma, surprised. She picked up a pawful of the cotton wool and looked at it. "I wonder if it's grown out of the ground," she said, "or fallen from the sky. If this all came down at once, how very uncomfortable it must have been!"

The Mymble went past with a tree across her toboggan chair.

"So you've awakened at last," she said casually. "Be sure you find a tree before it gets dark."

"But why...?" began Moominpappa.

"Too busy to stop now," shouted the Mymble over her shoulder and hurried on.

"Evidently you need a tree to be safe," Moominpappa said thoughtfully. "And the peril is coming tonight. She didn't even have time to say hello... It baffles me what it's all about."

"I can't understand it either," said Moominmamma thoughtfully, "but do put on your warm socks and scarves when you go to fetch that tree, and I'll try to get a little fire going in the stove meanwhile."

They walked off cautiously with stiff legs, keeping a close watch on the sky. You could not be sure that another load of cotton wool would not come tumbling down.

Moominpappa decided that, in spite of the threatening catastrophe, he would not cut down one of his own trees – they were too precious. Instead, the family climbed over the Fillyjonk's fence and selected a big tree that they decided would be of no further use to her, anyway.

"Do you think we're meant to hide in it?" asked Moomintroll.

"I don't know," said Moominpappa and continued chopping. "I don't understand it at all."

They had nearly reached the river with their tree, when the Fillyjonk came rushing towards them with her arms full of bags and parcels. She was red in the face and, thanks be, too hurried and flurried to recognise her own tree.

"Oh! bother!" cried the Fillyjonk. "Ill-bred hedgehogs simply shouldn't be *allowed* to... As I was saying to Gaffsie just now, it's an absolute disgrace..."

"The tree," said Moominpappa, clinging desperately to the Fillyjonk's fur collar, "what *are* we supposed to do with our tree?"

"The tree," repeated the Fillyjonk, bewildered, "the tree? Oh, how dreadful! What an awful bore... It's got to be dressed, of course... How on earth shall I get it done in time..."

She dropped her parcels in the snow, her bonnet slipped forward over her nose and she nearly burst into tears in her agitation.

Moominpappa shook his head and picked up the tree again.

2

At home Moominmamma had cleared the snow from the verandah, got out the life-belt, the aspirin and Moominpappa's rifle, and had made hot fomentations. You never could tell...

A little Squeak was sitting on the very edge of the sofa, drinking tea. It had sat in the snow under the verandah, looking so miserable that Moominmamma had asked it in.

"Well, here's the tree," said Moominpappa. "I only wish we knew what it's going to be used for. The Fillyjonk said it's supposed to be dressed."

"We haven't got such big clothes," said Moominmamma, worried. "What could she have meant?"

"Isn't it beautiful!" exclaimed the little Squeak, swallowing its tea the wrong way from sheer nervousness, and was instantly sorry it had dared to raise its voice.

"Do *you* know how to dress a tree?" asked the Snork Maiden.

The Squeak went as red as a beetroot and whispered: "With pretty things. As prettily as you can. That's what I've heard." Then it was overwhelmed by

shyness, threw its paws over its face, upsetting the teacup at the same time, and rushed to disappear through the verandah door.

"Now you must all be quiet, because I'm thinking," said Moominpappa. "If the tree is to be made as beautiful as possible we can't be meant to hide in it, but it's to *pacify* the peril. I'm beginning to understand what it's all about."

They immediately carried the tree into the garden, planted it firmly in the snow, and began to dress it from top to bottom with all the most beautiful things they could think of. They decorated it with the shells from the summer flower beds and with the Snork Maiden's pearl necklace. They took down the crystals from the drawing-room chandelier and hung them on the branches, and at the top they put a red silk rose which Moominpappa had given to Moominmamma. Everyone brought the most beautiful things they could think of to appease the mysterious powers of the winter season.

When the tree was ready the Mymble came past again with her toboggan. This time she was going in the opposite direction and was, if possible, in an even greater hurry.

"Have you seen our Christmas tree?" Moomintroll called out.

"Heaven preserve us!" said the Mymble... "But then you've always been oddities... I've got to be off... must cook some food for Christmas."

"Food for Christmas," repeated Moomintroll, astonished. "Does it have to be fed, too?"

The Mymble hardly listened. "Do you think one can do without food for Christmas?" she said impatiently and kicked off with her toboggan down the slope.

Moominmamma spent all afternoon bustling round, and just before twilight the Christmas's food was ready and arranged in small cups round the tree. There was fruit juice, yoghourt, bilberry pie, eggs and various other things that the Moomin family liked. "Do you think the Christmas is *very* hungry?" asked Moominmamma anxiously.

"He could hardly be hungrier than I am," said Moominpappa, looking at the food longingly; but little creatures must always be very polite to the great powers of nature. He sat shivering in the snow with the quilt drawn right up over his ears.

In the valley below, lights were appearing in all the windows. They shone under the trees and on the branches, and flickering beams darted here and there across the snow.

Moomintroll looked at his pappa meaningfully.

"All right," said Moominpappa, "to be on the safe side."

So Moomintroll went into the house and collected up all the candles he could find. He pushed them into the snow round the tree and lit them carefully, one by one, until they were all burning – to pacify the darkness and the Christmas.

Little by little, silence fell on the valley – maybe everyone had returned home to sit and wait for the coming peril.

Only one solitary shadowy figure was still to be seen, running among the trees – it was the Hemulen.

"Hello," called Moomintroll softly. "Is it coming soon?"

"Don't distract me," said the Hemulen gruffly. His nose was deep in a long list of things with nearly everything crossed out. He sat down by one of the candles and began to work through it. "Mamma, Pappa, Gaffsie," he murmured. "All the cousins... the eldest hedgehog... the little ones don't need anything... and Sniff didn't give me anything last year... Misable and Whomper and Auntie... this is driving me crazy."

"What's the matter?" asked the Snork Maiden anxiously.

"Presents," exclaimed the Hemulen. "More and more presents every Christmas."

In a great hurry, he crossed something off his list and rushed away.

"Wait!" called Moomintroll. "Explain... and your gloves..."

But the Hemulen disappeared into the darkness, in a hurry like everyone else, and flustered because Christmas was coming.

The Moomin family went quietly into the house to look for presents.

Moominpappa chose his best trolling-spoon for pike, which lay in a very

55

pretty box. On it he wrote "To Christmas", and then he put it out in the snow. The Snork Maiden pulled off her anklet, and with a sigh she wrapped it up in tissue-paper.

And Moominmamma opened her most secret drawer and brought out the book with pictures – the only picture book in the whole valley.

What Moomintroll wrapped up was so precious and so private that no one was allowed to see it – and not even later, in the spring, did he disclose what he had given away. Then they all sat down in the snow and waited for the catastrophe.

Time went by, but nothing happened.

Only the little Squeak, who had been drinking tea, appeared from behind the woodshed. It had brought all its relations and their friends; and they were all just as small and grey and shrivelled and cold as he was.

"Happy Christmas," whispered the Squeak shyly.

"You're the first one to think that Christmas is happy," said Moominpappa. "Aren't you afraid of what's going to happen when it comes?"

"But it's here," murmured the Squeak and settled down in the snow with its relations.

"May we have a look? You've got such a wonderful tree!"

"And look at all the food!" said one of the relations longingly.

"And real presents!" said another relation.

"All my life I've been dreaming of seeing this close to," added the Squeak with a sigh.

Moominmamma moved closer to Moominpappa:

"Don't you think...?" she whispered.

"Yes, but supposing..." objected Moominpappa.

"Never mind," said Moomintroll. "If the Christmas is angry, perhaps we can escape to the verandah."

And he turned to the Squeak and said:

"Please help yourselves; it's all yours."

The Squeak could not believe its ears. Slowly it advanced towards the tree, and the long line of relations followed, their whiskers trembling with awe.

They had never had a Christmas of their own before.

"I think we'd better be off," said Moominpappa anxiously.

Quickly they padded off to the verandah and hid under the table. Nothing happened. Cautiously they began to look out through the window.

Little Squeaks were sitting out there, eating and drinking, and opening presents and having more fun than they had ever had in their lives before. Finally they climbed up into the tree and fixed the lighted candles on all the branches.

"But I think there ought to be a big star at the top," said the Squeak's paternal aunt.

"Do you?" said the Squeak, looking thoughtfully at Moominmamma's red silk rose. "Does it really matter, so long as the intention's good?"

"Yes, we *ought* to have got a star," whispered Moominmamma. "But, of course, it's impossible."

They looked up at the sky, so black and distant, but incredibly full of stars – a thousand times more full than in the summer. And the biggest of them all stood right above the top of their tree.

"I'm rather sleepy," said Moominmamma. "And I'm too tired to think any more about the meaning of all this; but it seems to be turning out all right."

"In any case, I'm not afraid of Christmas now," said Moomintroll. "I think the Hemulen and the Mymble and the Fillyjonk must have got things mixed up, somehow."

And they put the Hemulen's yellow gloves on the verandah railing to make sure that he would find them, and went inside to continue their long sleep while they waited for spring to come again.

No, Ivy, No

No, Ivy, no,
  It must not be, indeed;
Let Holly have the mastery,
  It's always been agreed.

Holly stands in the hall,
  Lovely to behold;
Ivy stands outside the door,
  Where she's sorely cold.
No, Ivy, no...

Holly and his merry men,
  They sing and dance and leap;
Ivy and her maidens,
  They wring their hands and weep.
No, Ivy, no...

Ivy has a chilblain,
  She caught it from the cold,
So all Ivy's maids are caught
  Who don't do as they're told.
No, Ivy, no...

Holly has berries
  As red as any rose,
The forester and hunter
  Keep them from the does.
No, Ivy, no...

Ivy has berries
  As black as hedgerow sloes,
There comes the owl
  Who eats them as she goes.
No, Ivy, no...

Holly brings the birds,
  A very pretty flock –
The nightingale, the woodpecker,
  And the gentle lark.
No, Ivy, no...

So tell me, good Ivy,
  Just what birds have you?
Only the little owl
  Who cries to-whit to-woo!

No, Ivy, no,
  It must not be, indeed;
Let Holly have the mastery,
  It's always been agreed.

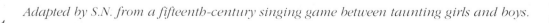

Adapted by S.N. from a fifteenth-century singing game between taunting girls and boys.

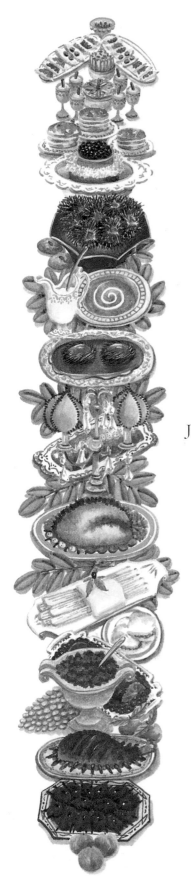

ESCOFFIER
CHRISTMAS MENU, 1906

Frivolité

Caviar frais – Blinis de Sarrasin

Oursins de la Méditerranée

Natives au Raifort

Les Délices de St. Antoine

Tortue Verte

Velouté de Poulet aux nids d'hirondelle

Sterlet du Volga à la Moscovite

Barquette de Laitance à la Vénitienne

Chapon fin aux Perles du Périgord

Cardon épineux à la Toulousaine

Selle de Venaison aux Cerises

Crème de marrons

Jeune agneau piqué de sauge à la Provençais

Sylphides de Roitelets

Gelée de Pommes d'Amour aux Ecrevisses

Fine Champagne, 1820

Mandarines givrées

Cailles sous la cendre aux raisins

Bécassines rosées au feu de sarments

Salade Isabelle

Asperges de France

Foie gras poché au Vin de Moselle

Bûche de Noël en Surprise

Plum Pudding – Mince Pie

Mignardises aux violettes

Étoile du Berger

Fruits de Serre chaude

Café Turc

Grandes Liqueurs

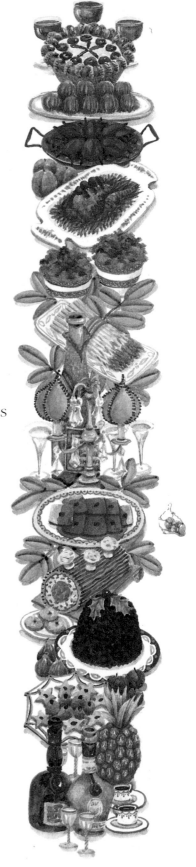

CHRISTMAS AT THE CRATCHITS'

from A Christmas Carol *by Charles Dickens (1812-1870)*

Such a bustle ensued that you might have thought a goose the rarest of all birds; a feathered phenomenon, to which a black swan was a matter of course – and, in truth, it was something very like it in that house. Mrs Cratchit made the gravy (ready beforehand in a little saucepan) hissing hot; Master Peter mashed the potatoes with incredible vigour; Miss Belinda sweetened up the apple sauce; Martha dusted the hot plates; Bob took Tiny Tim beside him in a tiny corner at the table; the two young Cratchits set chairs for everybody, not forgetting themselves, and, mounting guard upon their posts, crammed spoons into their mouths, lest they should shriek for goose before their turn came to be helped. At last the dishes were set on, and grace was said. It was succeeded by a breathless pause, as Mrs Cratchit, looking slowly all along the carving-knife, prepared to plunge it in the breast; but when she did, and when the long-expected gush of stuffing issued forth, one murmur of delight arose all round the board, and even Tiny Tim, excited by the two young Cratchits, beat on the table with the handle of his knife and feebly cried Hurrah!

There never was such a goose. Bob said he didn't believe there ever was such a goose cooked. Its tenderness and flavour, size and cheapness, were the themes of universal admiration. Eked out by apple sauce and mashed potatoes, it was a sufficient dinner for the whole family; indeed, as Mrs Cratchit

said with great delight (surveying one small atom of a bone upon the dish), they hadn't ate it all at last! Yet every one had had enough, and the youngest Cratchits, in particular, were steeped in sage and onion to the eyebrows! But now, the plates being changed by Miss Belinda, Mrs Cratchit left the room alone – too nervous to bear witnesses – to take the pudding up, and bring it in.

Suppose it should not be done enough! Suppose it should break in turning out! Suppose somebody should have got over the wall of the back-yard and stolen it, while they were merry with the goose – a supposition at which the two young Cratchits became livid! All sorts of horrors were supposed.

Hallo! A great deal of steam! The pudding was out of the copper. A smell like a washing-day! That was the cloth. A smell like an eating-house and a pastry-cook's next door to each other, with a laundress's next door to that! That was the pudding! In half a minute Mrs Cratchit entered – flushed, but smiling proudly – with the pudding, like a speckled cannon-ball, so hard and firm, blazing in half of half-a-quartern of ignited brandy, and bedight with Christmas holly stuck into the top.

Oh, a wonderful pudding! Bob Cratchit said, and calmly too, that he regarded it as the greatest success achieved by Mrs Cratchit since their marriage. Mrs Cratchit said that, now the weight was off her mind, she would confess she had her doubts about the quantity of flour. Everybody had something to say about it, but nobody said or thought it was at all a small pudding for a large family. It would have been flat heresy to do so. Any Cratchit would have blushed to hint at such a thing.

At last the dinner was all done, the cloth was cleared, the hearth swept, and the fire made up. The compound in the jug being tasted and considered perfect, apples and oranges were put upon the table and a shovel full of chestnuts on the fire. Then all the Cratchit family drew round the hearth in what Bob Cratchit called a circle, meaning half a one; and at Bob Cratchit's elbow stood the family display of glass. Two tumblers and a custard cup without a handle.

These held the hot stuff from the jug, however, as well as golden goblets would have done; and Bob served it out with beaming looks, while the chestnuts on the fire sputtered and cracked noisily. Then Bob proposed:

"A merry Christmas to us all, my dears. God bless us!"

Which all the family re-echoed.

"God bless us every one!" said Tiny Tim, the last of all.

CHRISTMAS DINNER

We were all sitting round the table.
There was roast turkey
there were roast potatoes
there were roast parsnips
there were broccoli tips
there was a dishful of crispy bacon off the turkey
there was wine, cider, lemonade
and milk for the youngsters.
Everything was set.
It was all on the table.
We were ready to begin.
Suddenly there was a terrible terrible scream.
Right next to the turkey was a worm.
A dirty little worm wriggling about like mad.

For a moment everyone looked at it.
Someone said very quietly, "Oh dear."
And everyone was thinking things like –
"How did it get there?"
"If that came out of the turkey,
I don't want any of it."
or
"I'm not eating any Christmas dinner. It could be full of
dirty little wriggly worms."

Now – as it happens,
I don't mind wriggly worms.
There was plenty of room for it
at the table.
It was just that... that...
no-one had asked it to come over
for Christmas dinner.

So I said,
"I don't think it came out of the turkey. I think –
It came off the bottom of the milk bottle."
And I picked up the worm,
and put it out the door to spend Christmas day
in a lovely patch of wet mud.
Much nicer place to be –
for a worm.

Michael Rosen

MRS PEPPERPOT'S CHRISTMAS

from Mrs Pepperpot's Year *by Alf Prøysen (1914-1970),*
translated by Marianne Helweg

One morning Mrs Pepperpot woke up and found she had shrunk. She climbed
to the top of the bed-post and swung her legs while she wondered what to do.

"What a nuisance!" she said. "Just when I wanted to go to the Christmas
Market with Mr Pepperpot!"

She wanted to buy a sheaf of corn for the birds' Christmas dinner, and she
wanted to get them a little bird-house where she could feed them every day.
The other thing she wanted was a wreath of mistletoe to hang over the door,
so that she could wish Mr Pepperpot a "Happy Christmas" with a kiss. But Mr
Pepperpot thought this was a silly idea.

"Quite unnecessary!" he said.

But Mrs Pepperpot was very clever at getting her own way; so even
though she was now no bigger than a mouse, she soon worked out a plan.
She heard her husband put his knapsack down on the floor in the kitchen and
she slid down the bed-post, scuttled over the doorstep and climbed into one
of the knapsack pockets.

Mr Pepperpot put the knapsack on his back and set off through the snow
on his kick-sledge, while Mrs Pepperpot peeped out from the pocket.

At the market there were crowds of people, both big and small; everyone shopping, and there was plenty to choose from! At one stall stood a farmer selling beautiful golden sheaves of corn. As her husband walked past the stall Mrs Pepperpot climbed out from the knapsack pocket and disappeared inside the biggest sheaf of all.

"Hello, Mr Pepperpot," said the farmer, "how about some corn for the birds this Christmas?"

"Too dear!" answered Mr Pepperpot gruffly.

"Oh no, it's not!" squeaked the little voice of Mrs Pepperpot. "If you don't buy this sheaf of corn I'll tell everyone you're married to the woman who shrinks!"

Now Mr Pepperpot above all hates people to know about his wife turning small, so when he saw her waving to him from the biggest sheaf he said to the farmer: "I've changed my mind; I'll have that one, please!"

But the farmer told him he would have to wait in the queue.

Only a little girl saw Mrs Pepperpot slip out of the corn and dash into a bird-house on Mr Andersen's stall. He was a carpenter and made all his bird-houses look just like real little houses with doors and windows for the birds to fly in and out. Of course Mrs Pepperpot chose the prettiest house; it even had curtains in the windows and from behind these she watched her husband buy the very best sheaf of corn and stuff it in his knapsack.

He thought his wife was safe inside and was just about to get on his kick-sledge and head for home, when he heard a little voice calling from the next stall.

"Hello, Husband!" squeaked Mrs Pepperpot. "Haven't you forgotten something? You were going to buy me a bird-house!"

Mr Pepperpot hurried over to the stall. He pointed to the house with the curtains and said: "I want to buy that one, please!"

Mr Andersen was busy with his customers. "You'll have to take your turn," he said.

So once more poor Mr Pepperpot had to stand patiently in a queue. He hoped that no one else would buy the house with his wife inside.

But she wasn't inside; she had run out of the back door, and now she was on her way to the next stall. Here there was a pretty young lady selling holly and mistletoe. Mrs Pepperpot had to climb up the post to reach the nicest wreath, and there she stayed hidden.

Soon Mr Pepperpot came by, carrying both the sheaf of corn and the little bird-house.

The young lady gave him a dazzling smile and said: "Oh, Mr Pepperpot, wouldn't you like to buy a wreath of mistletoe for your wife?"

"No thanks," said Mr Pepperpot, "I'm in a hurry."

"Swing high! Swing low! I'm in the mistletoe!" sang Mrs Pepperpot from her lofty perch.

When Mr Pepperpot caught sight of her his mouth fell open: "Oh dear!" he groaned. "This is too bad!"

With a shaking hand he paid the young lady the right money and lifted the wreath down himself, taking care that Mrs Pepperpot didn't slip out of his fingers. This time there would be no escape; he would take his wife straight home, whether she liked it or not. But just as he was leaving, the young lady said: "Oh, Sir, you're our one hundredth customer, so you get a free balloon!" and she handed him a red balloon.

Before anyone could say "Jack Robinson" Mrs Pepperpot had grabbed the string and, while Mr Pepperpot was struggling with his purse, gloves and parcels, his tiny wife was soaring up into the sky. Up she went over the marketplace, and soon she was fluttering over the trees of the forest, followed by a crowd of crows and magpies and small birds of every sort.

"Here I come!" she shouted in

bird-language. For, when Mrs Pepperpot was small, she could talk with animals and birds.

A big crow cawed: "Are you going to the moon with that balloon?"

"Not quite, I hope!" said Mrs Pepperpot, and she told them the whole story. The birds all squawked with glee when they heard about the corn and the bird-house she had got for them.

"But first you must help me," said Mrs Pepperpot. "I want you all to hang on to this balloon string and guide me back to land on my own doorstep."

So the birds clung to the string with their beaks and claws and, as they flew down to Mrs Pepperpot's house, the balloon looked like a kite with fancy bows tied to its tail.

When Mrs Pepperpot set foot on the ground she instantly grew to her normal size.

So she waved goodbye to the birds and went indoors to wait for Mr Pepperpot.

It was late in the evening before Mr Pepperpot came home, tired and miserable after searching everywhere for his lost wife. He put his knapsack down in the hall and carried the sheaf of corn and the bird-house outside. But when he came in again he noticed that the mistletoe had disappeared.

"Oh well," he said sadly, "what does it matter now that Mrs Pepperpot is gone?"

He opened the door into the kitchen; there was the mistletoe hanging over the doorway and, under it, as large as life, stood Mrs Pepperpot!

"Darling husband!" she said, as she put her arms round his neck and gave him a great big smacking kiss:

"Happy Christmas!"

Epstein, Spare That Yule Log!

When I was but a boy,
'Twas my once-a-yearly joy
To arise of a Yuletide morning,
And eagerly behold
The crimson and the gold
Of the messages the mantelpiece adorning.
There were angels, there were squires,
There were steeples, there were spires,
There were villagers, and mistletoe and holly,
There were cosy English inns
With the snow around their chins,
And I innocently thought them rather jolly.
I blush for me, but by your leave,
I'm afraid that I am still naïve.

Oh, give me an old-fashioned Christmas card,
With mistletoe galore, and holly by the yard,
With galumptious greens and gorgeous scarlets,
With crackling logs and apple-cheeked varlets,
With horses prancing down a frosty road,
And a stagecoach laden with a festive load,
And the light from the wayside windows streaming,
And a white moon rising and one star gleaming.

Departed is the time
Of Christmases sublime;
My soprano is now a mezzo-basso;
And the mantelpiece contains
The angular remains
Of a later representative Picasso.
There are circles, there are dots,
There are corners, there are spots,
There are modernistic snapshots of the city;
Or, when the artist lags,
They are livened up with gags.
You must choose between the arty and the witty.
I blush for me, but I must say
I wish you'd take them all away.

Oh, give me an old-fashioned Christmas card,
With hostlers hostling in an old inn yard,
With church bells chiming their silver notes,
And jolly red squires in their jolly red coats,
And a good fat goose by the fire that dangles,
And a few more angels and a few less angles.
Turn backward, Time, to please this bard,
And give me an old-fashioned Christmas card.

Ogden Nash (1902-1971)

CHRISTMAS IS COMING

Christmas is coming,
    The geese are getting fat,
Please to put a penny
    In the old man's hat.
If you haven't got a penny,
    A ha'penny will do;
If you haven't got a ha'penny,
    Then God bless you!

St Thomas's Day is past and gone,
And Christmas almost come,
    Maidens arise,
    And make your pies,
And save young Bobby some.

Christmas comes but once a year,
And when it comes it brings good cheer,
A pocket full of money, and a cellar full of beer.

Traditional

CHRISTMAS TREE

Up a heavy wooded hill
A brother and sister go
As on a new adventure,
Climbing through a foot of snow.

Their faces shine; their axe is gleaming.
All morning seems to be their nurture.
They inspect the winter world
As if they were out to conquer nature.

Hand and helve now have their will.
They cut a Christmas tree from earth,
Two children shouldering home the trophy
To give the tree symbolic birth.

Then worshipping, not knowing,
With lights, and games, and gifts, they play
Lightly, in their youthful growing,
Nor climb to confront divinity.

Richard Eberhart

WINTER POEM

Deep and crisp and even
The snow lay round about,
As we went walking
Through a Bohemian winter
On the untrodden ground.

The sun struck blue and silver
From the whiteness we walked
Till snow fell, and then
Through spires of trees
Angels and giants stalked.

Gerda Mayer

TIM RABBIT'S CHRISTMAS TREE

from The Adventures of No Ordinary Rabbit
by Alison Uttley (1884-1976)

Mrs Rabbit and her little son leaned out of the bedroom window one December night to look at the moon.

"Will it be fine tomorrow, Mother?" asked Tim.

Mrs Rabbit wrinkled her nose and then held her head up in the air, sniffing.

"I smell snow," said she. "Smell, Tim! Smell the snow, right up there in the sky, hidden in a cloud!"

Tim held up his small nose. Yes, there was the peculiar sweet icy smell which tells the countryman snow is coming.

"Hurrah!" he cried as he cuddled down into bed. "Hurrah for snowballs and skating and icicles, and —"

"And not much food, and cold feet, and little frozen birds," added Mrs Rabbit, solemnly, as she tucked him up and gave him a kiss on his whiskers.

The next day there was no need to smell, the ground was white with snow. The little larch trees in the plantation looked as if they had grown in a fairy-tale land. Some of the fir trees were so small that Tim Rabbit could nearly jump over them – that is, in fine weather, but now the snow had come he had to walk carefully till the frost made a hard surface for his feet.

Tim knew all about these little fir trees.

"These are Christmas trees," his mother had told him one day when they walked through the plantation, listening to the birds. "Just before Christmas the woodman comes and digs up many of these trees, and carts them to the towns. I never knew what happened to them there, but a tree came back last year, and was planted again. It told me all about its adventures."

"There it is," she continued, pointing to a neat small tree. "That's the tree which went away and returned. That little withered twig on the top is where the star hung, and that burnt twig is where a candle set it alight for one terrible moment."

Tim Rabbit stared in amazement, and the tree bowed its head and murmured, "Yes, it's true, quite true."

"And there were spickles and sparkles and toys all over it, hanging from the branches," added Mrs Rabbit.

The tree nodded again. "Yes, it's true," it whispered. Then a bird flew down to the little Christmas tree, and Mrs Rabbit and Tim walked on.

Tim thought of this tree when the snow fell, and he ran out to the wood to look at it. Whilst he was sitting beneath its low branches which dipped almost to the ground, the woodman came, with his horse and cart and spade. Tim moved a little farther off and watched the man dig up some of the small trees. The Christmas tree was left behind for it had the disfigurement of the burnt twig.

"Aren't you sorry to be left?" asked Tim when the wood was silent again, and the creaking cart was far away. "Don't you wish you were going back to the town?"

The tree shook its branches so hard that the snow fell off. "No. No. No. No," it seemed to say.

On Christmas Eve Tim returned to the tree and it waved its branches to welcome him.

"Would you like to be a real Christmas tree again, fir tree," he asked, "if you could stay here?"

The tree nodded its branches till the stiff needles rattled like a peal of bells.

"Well, I'll go off and find a few things to decorate you," said Tim, and he scampered across the wood, looking to left and right as he ran.

Up in the beech tree sat the squirrel, who had come out for a breath of air.

"Hello, Squirrel," called Tim. "Can you give me a few odds and ends for my Christmas tree?"

"Are you going to have a tree, Tim? Certainly I will find something." She came down the tree and hunted in her store-cupboard among the roots. She brought out a fistful of nuts, little wood nuts from the hazel trees. Tim put them in his pocket, thanked her, and ran on.

After a while he met Mr Hare, who was lolloping at a great rate.

Mr Hare lifted his eyebrows in surprise when Tim asked him for something for his Christmas tree.

"Christmas tree?" he echoed. "The woods are full of Christmas trees." But when he saw Tim's disappointed face he pulled a turnip out of his pocket.

"Here's a watch you can have, Tim. It goes if you shake it, and when it stops you can eat it!"

"Thank you, Mr Hare," laughed Tim, shaking the turnip, and listening to the imaginary tick-tock. "This is beautiful. I never knew that you could tell the time by a turnip," and he put it in his pocket and ran on.

After a while he saw a cock pheasant, stalking proudly through the snow.

"Excuse me, sir," said Tim politely. "Have you such a thing as a Christmas present about you?"

The pheasant opened wide its fierce eye, and gazed at Tim.

"What have you done to deserve a present?" it asked.

"I've run up and down the woods and commons every day, enjoying myself," said Tim. "I'm no ordinary rabbit."

"Ha! Well, take this feather," said the pheasant, drawing a lovely long plume from its tail. "It will serve to remind you of the truly great ones of the earth," and the bird stalked on, leaving Tim overwhelmed with happiness.

He called at the farmhouse, where the white hen gave him a couple of eggs, and the cock brought out a basket of corn. The duck gave a quill pen, and the cow a wee bottle of milk. The sheep produced a woolly blanket, and the old mare let him take a few hairs from her tail to tie up the presents.

Then Tim went back to the tree, which stood all white and lonely in the wood.

He hung the nuts all round the branches, as if they were growing, and slung the eggs from a bough. He stuck the bright feather on one branch, and the quill on another. He put the woolly blanket, the turnip, and the bottle of milk on the lowest branches, and tied them there with the horse-hairs. Then on the ground he sprinkled the corn, for the tiny creatures of the wood.

There was only one thing missing, and that was a star to hang on the topmost bough of the tree. He stood back to admire his work, for night was falling, and it was time to go home. But what do you think he saw? One of the golden stars of heaven was peeping through the top branch, just as if it belonged there!

Tim ran home to the little house on the common as fast as he could.

"Oh, Mother, Mother!" he cried. "A happy Christmas tomorrow! Come and look at my Christmas tree, which I've made for all the wood creatures."

Mrs Rabbit ran back with him to the wood, to look at the tree which stood radiant in the starlight. Then she hugged her little rabbit.

"You are the best surprise of all," said she, and the Christmas tree nodded its branches, very gently, lest the presents should fall off, and murmured, "Very true!"

THE CHRISTMAS TREE

Put out the lights now!
Look at the Tree, the rough tree dazzled
In oriole plumes of flame,
Tinselled with twinkling frost fire, tasselled
With stars and moons – the same
That yesterday hid in the spinney and had no fame
Till we put out the lights now.

Hard are the nights now:
The fields at moonrise turn to agate,
Shadows are cold as jet;
In dyke and furrow, in copse and faggot
The frost's tooth is set;
And stars are the sparks whirled out by the
    north wind's fret
On the flinty nights now.

So feast your eyes now
On mimic star and moon-cold bauble:
Worlds may wither unseen,
But the Christmas Tree is a tree of fable,
A phoenix in evergreen,
And the world cannot change or chill what
    its mysteries mean
To your hearts and eyes now.

The vision dies now
Candle by candle: the tree that embraced it
Returns to its own kind,
To be earthed again and weather as best it
May the frost and the wind.
Children, it too had its hour –
    you will not mind
If it lives or dies now.

C. Day Lewis (1904-1972)

JOY AND GIVING

As I Sat On a Sunny Bank

As I sat on a sunny bank
On Christmas day in the morning,
I saw three ships come sailing by
On Christmas day in the morning.
And who do you think were in those ships
But Joseph and his fair lady:
He did whistle and she did sing,
And all the bells on earth did ring
For joy our Saviour He was born
On Christmas day in the morning.

Anon

CHRISTMAS BELLS

I heard the bells on Christmas day
Their old familiar carols play,
    And wild and sweet
    The words repeat
Of "Peace on earth, good will to men!"

And thought how, as the day had come,
The belfries of all Christendom
    Had rolled along
    The unbroken song,
Of "Peace on earth, good will to men!"

Till ringing, singing on its way,
The world revolved from night to day –
    A voice, a chime
    A chant sublime,
Of "Peace on earth, good will to men!"

And in despair I bowed my head;
"There is no peace on earth," I said,
    "For hate is strong
    And mocks the song
Of peace on earth, good will to men!"

Then pealed the bells more loud and deep:
"God is not dead; nor doth he sleep!
    The wrong shall fail,
    The right prevail,
With peace on earth, good will to men!"

Henry Wadsworth Longfellow (1807-1882)

THE MERRY BELLS OF YULE

The time draws near the birth of Christ:
    The moon is hid; the night is still;
    The Christmas bells from hill to hill
Answer each other in the mist.

Four voices of four hamlets round,
    From far and near, on mead and moor,
    Swell out and fail, as if a door
Were shut between me and the sound;

Each voice four changes on the wind,
    That now dilate and now decrease,
    Peace and goodwill, goodwill and peace,
Peace and goodwill, to all mankind.

This year I slept and woke with pain,
    I almost wished no more to wake,
    And that my hold on life would break
Before I heard those bells again;

But they my troubled spirit rule,
    For they controlled me when a boy;
    They bring me sorrow touched with joy,
The merry, merry bells of Yule.

Lord Tennyson (1809-1892)
from In Memoriam

SINGING IN THE STREETS

I had almost forgotten the singing in the streets,
Snow piled up by the houses, drifting
Underneath the door into the warm room,
Firelight, lamplight, the little lame cat
Dreaming in soft sleep on the hearth, mother dozing,
Waiting for Christmas to come, the boys and me
Trudging over blanket fields waving lanterns to the sky.
I had almost forgotten the smell, the feel of it all,
The coming back home, with girls laughing like stars,
Their cheeks, holly berries, me kissing one,
Silent-tongued, soberly, by the long church wall;
Then back to the kitchen table, supper on the white cloth,
Cheese, bread, the home-made wine:
Symbols of the Night's joy, a holy feast.
And I wonder now, years gone, mother gone,
The boys and girls scattered, drifted away with the snowflakes,
Lamplight done, firelight over,
If the sounds of our singing in the streets are still there,
Those old tunes, still praising:
And now, a life-time of Decembers away from it all,
A branch of remembering holly spears my cheeks,
And I think it may be so;
Yes, I believe it may be so.

Leonard Clark

THE WICKED SINGERS

And have you been out carol singing,
Collecting for the Old Folks' Dinner?

Oh yes indeed, oh yes indeed.

And did you sing all the Christmas numbers,
Every one a winner?

Oh yes indeed, oh yes indeed.

Good King Wenceslas, and Hark
The Herald Angels Sing?

Oh yes indeed, oh yes indeed.

And did you sing them loud and clear
And make the night sky ring?

Oh yes indeed, oh yes indeed.

And did you count up all the money?
Was it quite a lot?

Oh yes indeed, oh yes indeed.

And did you give it all to the Vicar,
Everything you'd got?

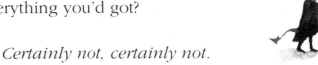

Certainly not, certainly not.

Kit Wright

Just Like Old Times

from The Wind in the Willows
by Kenneth Grahame (1859-1922)

"The field mice go round carol-singing regularly at this time of the year," said the Mole. "They're quite an institution in these parts. And they never pass me over – they come to Mole End last of all; and I used to give them hot drinks, and supper too sometimes, when I could afford it. It will be like old times to hear them again."

"Let's have a look at them!" cried the Rat, jumping up and running to the door.

It was a pretty sight, and a seasonable one, that met their eyes when they flung the door open. In the fore-court, lit by the dim rays of a horn lantern, some eight or ten little field-mice stood in a semicircle, red worsted comforters round their throats, their forepaws thrust deep into their pockets, their feet jigging for warmth. With bright beady eyes they glanced shyly at each other, sniggering a little, sniffing and applying coat-sleeves a good deal. As the door opened, one of the elder ones that carried the lantern was just saying, "Now then, one, two, three!" and forthwith their shrill little voices uprose on the air, singing one of the old-time carols that their forefathers composed in fields that were fallow and held by frost, or when snow-bound in chimney corners, and handed down to be sung in the miry street to lamp-lit windows at Yule-time.

CAROL

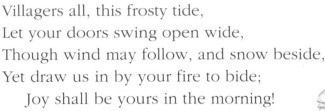

Villagers all, this frosty tide,
Let your doors swing open wide,
Though wind may follow, and snow beside,
Yet draw us in by your fire to bide;
   Joy shall be yours in the morning!

Here we stand in the cold and the sleet,
Blowing fingers and stamping feet,
Come from far away you to greet –
You by the fire and we in the street –
   Bidding you joy in the morning!

For ere one half of the night was gone,
Sudden a star has led us on,
Raining bliss and benison –
Bliss to-morrow and more anon,
   Joy for every morning!

Goodman Joseph toiled through the snow –
Saw the star o'er a stable low;
Mary she might not further go –
Welcome thatch, and litter below!
   Joy was hers in the morning!

And then they heard the angels tell
"Who were the first to cry Nowell?
Animals all, as it befell,
In the stable where they did dwell!
   Joy shall be theirs in the morning!"

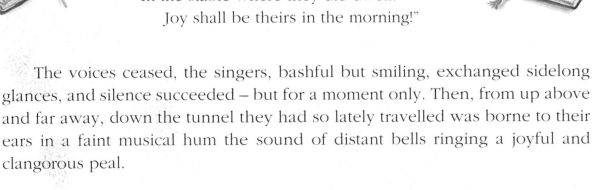

   The voices ceased, the singers, bashful but smiling, exchanged sidelong glances, and silence succeeded – but for a moment only. Then, from up above and far away, down the tunnel they had so lately travelled was borne to their ears in a faint musical hum the sound of distant bells ringing a joyful and clangorous peal.

"Very well sung, boys!" cried the Rat heartily. "And now come along in, all of you, and warm yourselves by the fire, and have something hot!"

"Yes, come along, field-mice," cried the Mole eagerly. "This is quite like old times! Shut the door after you. Pull up that settle to the fire."...

The field-mice, perched in a row on the settle, their small legs swinging, gave themselves up to enjoyment of the fire, and toasted their chilblains till they tingled; while the Mole, failing to draw them into easy conversation, plunged into family history and made each of them recite the names of his numerous brothers, who were too young, it appeared, to be allowed to go out a-carolling this year, but looked forward very shortly to winning the parental consent.

The Rat, meanwhile, was busy examining the label on one of the beer-bottles. "I perceive this to be Old Burton," he remarked approvingly. "*Sensible* Mole! The very thing! Now we shall be able to mull some ale! Get the things ready, Mole, while I draw the corks."

It did not take long to prepare the brew and thrust the tin heater well into the red heart of the fire; and soon every field-mouse was sipping and coughing and choking (for a little mulled ale goes a long way) and wiping his eyes and laughing and forgetting he had ever been cold in all his life.

GHOST STORY

Bring out the tall tales now that we told
by the fire as the gaslight bubbled like a diver.
Ghosts whooed like owls in the long nights
when I dared not look over my shoulder; animals
lurked in the cubbyhole under the stairs where the
gas meter ticked. And I remember that we went
singing carols once, when there wasn't the shaving
of a moon to light the flying streets. At the end
of a long road was a drive that led to a large
house, and we stumbled up the darkness of the drive
that night, each one of us afraid, each one holding
a stone in his hand in case, and all of us too brave
to say a word. The wind through the trees
made noises as of old and unpleasant and maybe
webfooted men wheezing in caves. We reached
the black bulk of the house.
"What shall we give them? Hark the Herald?"
"No," Jack said, "Good King Wenceslas.
I'll count three."
One, two, three, and we began to sing,
our voices high and seemingly distant in the
snow-felted darkness around the house that
was occupied by nobody we knew. We stood
close together, near the dark door.
"Good King Wenceslas looked out
On the Feast of Stephen..."
And then a small, dry voice, like the voice
of someone who has not spoken for a long time,
joined our singing: a small dry eggshell voice
from the other side of the door: a small dry voice
through the keyhole. And when we stopped running
we were outside *our* house; the front room was lovely:
balloons floated under the hot-water-bottle-gulping gas;
everything was good again and shone over the town.

"Perhaps it was a ghost," Jim said.
"Perhaps it was trolls," Dan said,
who was always reading.

"Let's go in and see if there's any jelly left,"
Jack said. And we did that.

Dylan Thomas (1914-1953)

THE SINGERS

We heard them leave our neighbours and draw nearer,
Easing their rough throats. One had a wicked cough.
Another could hardly have made his purpose clearer –
Give them Noel, collect, and then push off.

But on our doorstep they assumed politeness,
Whispered, fell silent, let the song begin,
And all we had lost was kindled by its brightness
Shrill as heartache, crying to come in.

John Mole

VILLAGE CAROLS
BETWEEN THE WARS

from Cider with Rosie *by Laurie Lee*

The week before Christmas, when snow seemed to lie thickest, was the moment for carol-singing; and when I think back to those nights it is to the crunch of snow and to the lights of the lanterns on it. Carol-singing in my village was a special tithe for the boys, the girls had little to do with it. Like hay-making, blackberrying, stone-clearing, and wishing-people-a-happy-Easter, it was one of our seasonal perks.

By instinct we knew just when to begin it; a day too soon and we should have been unwelcome, a day too late and we should have received lean looks from people whose bounty was already exhausted. When the true moment came, exactly balanced, we recognised it and were ready.

So as soon as the wood had been stacked in the oven to dry for the morning fire, we put on our scarves and went out through the streets, calling loudly between our hands, till the various boys who knew the signal ran out from their houses to join us.

One by one they came stumbling over the snow, swinging their lanterns around their heads, shouting and coughing horribly.

"Coming carol-barking then?"

We were the Church Choir, so no answer was necessary. For a year we had praised the Lord out of key, and as a reward for this service – on top of the Outing – we now had the right to visit all the big houses, to sing our carols and collect our tribute.

To work them all in meant a five-mile foot journey over wild and generally snowed-up country. So the first thing we did was to plan our route; a formality, as the route never changed. All the same, we blew on our fingers and argued; and then we chose our Leader. This was not binding, for we all fancied ourselves as Leaders, and he who started the night in that position usually trailed home with a bloody nose.

Eight of us set out that night. There was Sixpence the Tanner, who had never sung in his life (he just worked his mouth in church); the brothers Horace and Boney, who were always fighting everybody and always getting the worst of it; Clergy Green, the preaching maniac; Walt the bully, and my two brothers. As we went down the lane other boys, from other villages, were already about the hills, bawling "Kingwenslush", and shouting through keyholes "Knock on the knocker! Ring at the Bell! Give us a penny for singing so well!" They weren't an approved charity as we were, the Choir; but competition was in the air.

Our first call as usual was the house of the Squire, and we trouped nervously down his drive. For light we had candles in marmalade-jars suspended on loops of string, and they threw pale gleams on the towering snowdrifts that stood on each side of the drive. A blizzard was blowing, but we were well wrapped up, with Army puttees on our legs, woollen hats on our heads, and several scarves around our ears.

As we approached the Big House across its white silent lawns, we too grew respectfully silent. The lake near by was stiff and black, the waterfall frozen and still. We arranged ourselves shuffling around the big front door, then knocked and announced the Choir.

A maid bore the tidings of our arrival away into the echoing distances of the house, and while we waited we cleared our throats noisily. Then she came back, and the door was left ajar for us, and we were bidden to begin. We brought no music, the carols were in our heads. "Let's give 'em 'Wild Shepherds'," said Jack. We began in confusion, plunging into a

wreckage of keys, of different words and tempo; but we gathered our strength, he who sang loudest took the rest of us with him, and the carol took shape if not sweetness.

This huge stone house, with its ivied walls, was always a mystery to us. What were those gables, those rooms and attics, those narrow windows veiled by the cedar trees. As we sang "Wild Shepherds" we craned our necks, gaping into that lamplit hall which we had never entered; staring at the muskets and untenanted chairs, the great tapestries furred by dust – until suddenly, on the stairs, we saw the old Squire himself standing and listening with his head on one side.

He didn't move until we'd finished; then slowly he tottered towards us, dropped two coins in our box with a trembling hand, scratched his name in the book we carried, gave us each a long look with his moist blind eyes, then turned away in silence.

As though released from a spell, we took a few sedate steps, then broke into a run for the gate. We didn't stop till we were out of the grounds. Impatient, at last, to discover the extent of his bounty, we squatted by the cowsheds, held our lanterns over the book, and saw that he had written, "Two Shillings". This was quite a good start. No one of any worth in the district would dare to give us less than the Squire.

So with money in the box, we pushed on up the valley, pouring scorn on each other's performance. Confident now, we began to consider our quality and whether one carol was not better suited to us than another. Horace, Walt said, shouldn't sing at all; his voice was beginning to break. Horace disputed this and there was a brief token battle – they fought as they walked, kicking up divots of snow, then they forgot it, and Horace still sang.

Steadily we worked through the length of the valley, going from house to house, visiting the lesser and the greater gentry – the farmers, the doctors, the merchants, the majors, and other exalted persons. It was freezing hard and blowing too; yet not for a moment did we feel the cold. The snow blew into our faces, into our eyes and mouths, soaked through our puttees, got into our boots, and dripped from our woollen caps. But we did not care. The collecting-box grew heavier, and the list of names in the book longer and more extravagant, each trying to outdo the other.

Mile after mile we went, fighting against the wind, falling into snowdrifts, and navigating by the lights of the houses. And yet we never saw our audience. We called at house after house; we sang in courtyards and porches,

outside windows, or in the damp gloom of hallways; we heard voices from hidden rooms; we smelt rich clothes and strange hot food; we saw maids bearing in dishes or carrying away coffee cups; we received nuts, cakes, figs, preserved ginger, dates, cough-drops, and money; but we never once saw our patrons. We sang as it were at the castle walls, and apart from the Squire, who had shown himself to prove that he was still alive, we never expected it otherwise.

As the night drew on there was trouble with Boney. "Noël", for instance, had a rousing harmony which Boney persisted in singing, and singing flat. The others forbade him to sing it at all, and Boney said he would fight us. Picking himself up, he agreed we were right, then he disappeared altogether. He just turned away and walked into the snow and wouldn't answer when we called him back. Much later, as we reached a far point up the valley, somebody said "Hark!" and we stopped to listen. Far away across the fields from the distant village came the sound of a frail voice singing, singing "Noël", and singing it flat – it was Boney, branching out on his own.

We approached our last house high up on the hill, the place of Joseph the farmer. For him we had chosen a special carol, which was about the other Joseph, so that we always felt that singing it added a spicy cheek to the night. The last stretch of country to reach his farm was perhaps the most difficult of all. In these rough bare lanes, open to all winds, sheep were buried and wagons lost. Huddled together, we tramped in one another's footsteps, powdered snow blew into our screwed-up eyes, the candles burnt low, some blew out altogether, and we talked loudly above the gale.

Crossing, at last, the frozen mill-stream – whose wheel in summer still turned a barren mechanism – we climbed up to Joseph's farm. Sheltered by trees, warm on its bed of snow, it seemed always to be like this. As always it was late; as always this was our final call. The snow had a fine crust upon it, and the old trees sparkled like tinsel.

We grouped ourselves round the farmhouse porch. The sky cleared, and broad streams of stars ran down over the valley and away to Wales. On Slad's white slopes, seen through the black sticks of its woods, some red lamps still burned in the windows.

Everything was quiet; everywhere there was the faint crackling silence of the winter night. We started singing, and we were all moved by the words and the sudden trueness of our voices. Pure, very clear, and breathless we sang:

> As Joseph was a walking
> He heard an angel sing;
> "This night shall be the birth-time
> Of Christ the Heavenly King.
>
> He neither shall be bornèd
> In Housen nor in hall,
> Nor in a place of paradise
> But in an ox's stall..."

And two thousand Christmases became real to us then; the houses, the halls, the places of paradise had all been visited; the stars were bright to guide the Kings through the snow; and across the farmyard we could hear the beasts in their stalls. We were given roast apples and hot mince-pies, in our nostrils were spices like myrrh, and in our wooden box, as we headed back for the village, there were golden gifts for all.

THE WAITING GAME

Nuts and marbles in the toe,
An orange in the heel,
A Christmas stocking in the dark
Is wonderful to feel.

Shadowy, bulging length of leg
That crackles when you clutch,
A Christmas stocking in the dark
Is marvellous to touch.

You lie back on your pillow
But that shape's still hanging there.
A Christmas stocking in the dark
Is very hard to bear,

So try to get to sleep again
And chase the hours away.
A Christmas stocking in the dark
Must wait for Christmas Day.

John Mole

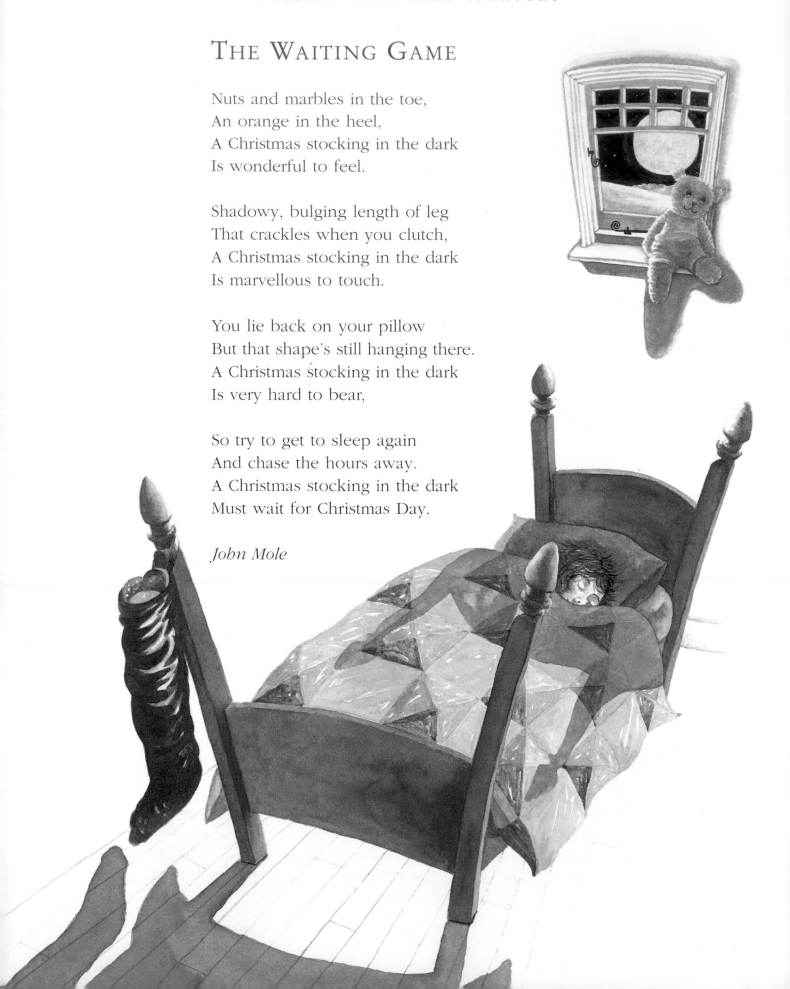

THE TREE THAT WENT MAD

from The Peculiar Triumph of Professor Branestawm
by Norman Hunter

There had never been a Christmas party at Professor Branestawm's house before. Because the Professor was always so immersed in thinking about new inventions he never had time left to think about old customs. But this time the Professor was absolutely going to have a Christmas party, because he had invented a present-giving invention.

"I have always thought, Dedshott," said the Professor to the Colonel, "that the, er, traditional Christmas tree offered possibilities for, um, development," by which of course he meant it could be interestingly fiddled about with.

"My idea," said the Professor, "consists of a purely automatic Christmas tree, fitted with a mechanical present distributor coupled to a greetings-speaking device and a gift wrapping attachment so that the, er, recipients receive their gifts suitably, um ah, wrapped up and accompanied by a Christmas greeting."

He pulled a lever, pressed some buttons and twiddled a twiddler.

Pop whizetty chugg chug. "Good King Wenceslas," sang the machine. "Look out!" cried the Professor. A highly decorative parcel shot out of the tree and landed on the Colonel's lap accompanied by a hearty "Happy Christmas!"

from the tree and "By Jove, what!" from the Colonel.

"Jolly clever, my word," he grunted. "How does it work, eh?"

The Professor didn't explain anything. He came over all coy and said, "Wait until my Christmas party, Dedshott."

The Professor's party started off all nice and ordinary, apart from the fact that it took place in November because the Professor couldn't wait to show off his invention. The guests arrived with presents for the Professor.

"Er, ah, thank you," said the Professor. "Now come this way please." He led the way down the passage, into the kitchen by mistake and nearly into the gas cooker and eventually after much pushing and excuse-me's they all got packed into his study where the automatic mechanical Christmas tree stood.

"Here is the present distributor," said the Professor, pointing to a row of eager-looking levers. "They are labelled with your names. All you have to, ah, do, is pull the lever with your name on."

"Marvellous!" cried the Colonel.

"Shall I declare the tree open?" said the Mayor and the Vicar, both at once. Then without waiting for an answer they both coughed and, in very high class voices, said, "I have pleasuah in declaring the tree open, hrrrmph."

Soon levers were being pulled, the machine was clanking away, the air was full of Christmas music and hearty greetings and the crash of paper parcels being excitably unwrapped.

The Mayor got a pair of silk stockings and a bottle of lavender water, which were really intended for Mrs Flittersnoop, because the Professor had got the names on the levers muddled up.

"Now that's what I call real kind," cried Mrs Flittersnoop, then she said "Oh!" in a rather pale voice when she found she had got a packet of corn cure and a tin of tobacco shaped like a pillar box, which should have gone to the postman.

Sister Aggie found herself with a box of cigars. The Vicar had a china doll with no clothes on. Colonel Dedshott's present was a yellow bonnet with imitation cherries on it. The Pagwell Library man got a packet of large square dog biscuits and wondered if they were a new kind of book.

"I fear there has been some mistake," murmured the Vicar. "May I be permitted to exchange this charming gift for something more suitable?" He pushed the china doll into the machine and pulled one of the levers. At the same time the Mayor and sister Aggie pushed their presents back and started pressing not-meant-to-be-pressed buttons, to change their presents.

"No no no!" cried the Professor, clashing his spectacles. But he was too late. The automatic Christmas tree evidently resented having its presents returned. It rang out a burst of Christmas bells that sounded like a fire engine, emitted a cloud of dirty green smoke, shouted, "Merry Christmas on the feast of Stephen!" and shot out of the house and down the road.

"After it!" roared the Colonel, who reckoned he knew how to deal with this situation. They all tore after the machine that was shouting a mixed version of "The Twelve Days of Christmas." Colonel Dedshott drew his sword and rushed at it. The machine took it away and returned it gift wrapped.

"Five golden things," sang the machine, careering down the road, giving out presents and Christmas wishes right and left. Three little boys with a November the fifth Guy who were asking for pennies got instead a parcel of files and screwdrivers that were the Professor's Christmas present for himself. A lady coming out of a supermarket was presented with the Vicar's china doll

and a yard and a half of "The Holly and the Ivy" sung out of tune.

"Dash round the other way and cut it off," shouted the Colonel to the driver of a steam roller. But steam rollers are absolutely no good at dashing.

The Professor flew past on his bicycle in hot pursuit, but the machine scattered a box of coloured marbles on the road and he side-slipped into the Mayor's arms.

"Thirty-five maids a dancing, ninety ladies singing, no end of a lot of swans splashing about, five golden rings," sang the machine. It tore down Uppington Street, round the Square, turned left into Wright Street, hotly pursued by the Professor, his guests and crowds of Pagwell people who were shouting, "Stop thief!" which was all they could think of to shout.

The machine ran out of presents and started picking up anything it could see and wrapping it in anything handy. A policeman held up his hand to make it stop and was given a piece of paving stone wrapped in an advertisement for second-hand bicycles.

On rushed the machine, across the High Street, smack into a smash-and-grab robber who was just dashing out of a jewellers' shop with a sack full of valuables.

"And a partridge up a gum tree," shouted the machine. It sat on the robber, tore open the sack and was only just stopped from handing out watches and pearl necklaces all round by the arrival of an absolute heap of policemen. They arrested the robber and would have arrested the machine too, only Professor Branestawm arrived just in time to turn off the works and explain what had happened, which the policemen didn't believe anyway.

"Disturbing the peace, y'know," said a police sergeant with three chins. "Conduct likely to cause..."

But the Professor and the Colonel between them had got the Christmas tree apart, packed it into a passing wheelbarrow, given a new fifty pence piece to the man who was pushing it and persuaded him to take it back to the Professor's house.

And everything turned out nicely because the jeweller gave the Professor a reward for catching the robber, so the Professor was able to buy some very handsome presents to give to everyone at Christmas, which he did by the very unoriginal but completely satisfactory method of handing them over and saying, "Happy um – ah – Christmas."

A GIFT FROM THE STARS

On Christmas Eve, on the first chime of midnight,
the Christmas King and Queen of Christmas
take the new moon, sharp as a blade,
and slit the thin paper sky.

They help each other wrap up the frosty stars
in the night's dark blue wrapping paper;
the Queen stretches out her sparkling hand
and grasps a passing comet to use as a gift tag.

The Queen of Christmas and the Christmas King
then take their present on a long journey:
     they slide past the icy meteorites,
     they glide between the glassy suns,
     they slink in and out of cosmic clouds,
     they skim the outer edges of planets' rings
making their way through the caves and caverns of space
to this shining Earth
to this cold country
to this snowy town
to this still street
to this sleeping house
to this quiet bedroom
to this soft bed
and place their sky gift on your pillow.

John Rice

KING JOHN'S CHRISTMAS

King John was not a good man –
    He had his little ways.
And sometimes no one spoke to him
    For days and days and days.
And men who came across him,
    When walking in the town,
Gave him a supercilious stare,
Or passed with noses in the air –
And bad King John stood dumbly there,
    Blushing beneath his crown.

King John was not a good man,
    And no good friends had he.
He stayed in every afternoon...
    But no one came to tea.
And, round about December,
    The cards upon his shelf
Which wished him lots of Christmas cheer,
And fortune in the coming year,
Were never from his near and dear,
    But only from himself.

King John was not a good man,
    Yet had his hopes and fears.
They'd given him no present now
    For years and years and years.
But every year at Christmas,
    While minstrels stood about,
Collecting tribute from the young
For all the songs they might have sung,
He stole away upstairs and hung
    A hopeful stocking out.

King John was not a good man,
    He lived his life aloof;
Alone he thought a message out
    While climbing up the roof.
He wrote it down and propped it
    Against the chimney stack:
"TO ALL AND SUNDRY – NEAR AND FAR –
F. CHRISTMAS IN PARTICULAR."
And signed it not "Johannes R."
    But very humbly, "JACK."

"I want some crackers,
    And I want some candy;
I think a box of chocolates
    Would come in handy;
I don't mind oranges,
    I do like nuts!
And I SHOULD like a pocket-knife
    That really cuts.
And, oh! Father Christmas, if you love me at all,
Bring me a big, red india-rubber ball!"

King John was not a good man –
    He wrote this message out,
And gat him to his room again,
    Descending by the spout.
And all that night he lay there,
    A prey to hopes and fears.
"I think that's him a-coming now,"
    (Anxiety bedewed his brow.)
"He'll bring one present, anyhow –
    The first I've had for years."

"Forget about the crackers,
    And forget about the candy;
I'm sure a box of chocolates
    Would never come in handy;
I don't like oranges,
    I don't want nuts,
And I HAVE got a pocket-knife
    That almost cuts.
But, oh! Father Christmas, if you love me at all,
Bring me a big, red india-rubber ball!"

King John was not a good man --
    Next morning when the sun
Rose up to tell a waiting world
    That Christmas had begun,
And people seized their stockings,
    And opened them with glee,
And crackers, toys and games appeared,
And lips with sticky sweets were smeared,
King John said grimly: "As I feared,
    Nothing again for me!"

"I did want crackers,
    And I did want candy;
I know a box of chocolates
    Would come in handy;
I do love oranges,
    I did want nuts.
I haven't got a pocket-knife –
    Not one that cuts.
And, oh! if Father Christmas had loved me at all,
He would have brought a big, red india-rubber ball!"

King John stood by the window,
And frowned to see below
The happy bands of boys and girls
All playing in the snow.
A while he stood there watching,
And envying them all...
When through the window big and red
There hurtled by his royal head,
And bounced and fell upon the bed,
An india-rubber ball!

AND OH, FATHER CHRISTMAS,
MY BLESSINGS ON YOU FALL
FOR BRINGING HIM
A BIG, RED,
INDIA-RUBBER
BALL!

A. A. Milne (1882-1956)

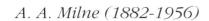

AFTERTHOUGHT

For weeks before it comes I feel excited, yet when it
At last arrives, things all go wrong:
My thoughts don't seem to fit.

I've planned what I'll give everyone and what they'll give to me,
And then on Christmas morning all
The presents seem to be

Useless and tarnished. I have dreamt that everything would come
To life – presents and people too.
Instead of that, I'm dumb,

And people say, "How horrid! What a sulky little boy!"
And they are right. I *can't* seem pleased.
The lovely shining toy

I wanted so much when I saw it in a magazine
Seems pointless now. And Christmas too
No longer seems to mean

The hush, the star, the baby, people being kind again.
The bells are rung, sledges are drawn,
And peace on earth for men.

Elizabeth Jennings

SIX THINGS FOR CHRISTMAS

I wish to be given beautiful things this Christmas,
Beautiful but impossible
For gifts that are fresh are nice
But the joy is soon gone
And only the physical volume remains
To be pleasantly taken for granted.
But if an object is lost
Then a small pain is born
And goes in search, beseeching,
To embrace the thing that was.
And should the thing be regiven
Then embraced with that small pain
It becomes a thing of beauty.

So, six things that once upon a time
I lost:
One: is a bald sad man I lost somewhere
Within my seventeenth year.
Two: was an acquaintance that I had with Mt. Kerinyaga,
Whom I also loved.
Three: a parcel of thoughts that I continually lose.
Four: a mouse called Nuisance that was all grey.
Five: a beautiful Aunt who gave me a sight
Of two grey heron when I was a boy.
Six: that thing we all lost so long ago – Christmas.

John May

MR EDWARDS
MEETS SANTA CLAUS

from Little House on the Prairie
by Laura Ingalls Wilder (1867-1957)

When Laura was a small girl, the Ingalls family trekked west in their covered wagon from the Big Woods of Wisconsin to the vast emptiness of the High Prairie. Mr Edwards, "a wild-cat from Tennessee", is their nearest neighbour, on the far side of the creek.

The days were short and cold, the wind whistled sharply, but there was no snow. Cold rains were falling. Day after day the rain fell, pattering on the roof and pouring from the eaves.

Mary and Laura stayed close by the fire, sewing their nine-patch quilt blocks, or cutting paper dolls from scraps of wrapping-paper, and hearing the wet sound of the rain. Every night was so cold that they expected to see snow next morning, but in the morning they saw only sad, wet grass.

They pressed their noses against the squares of glass in the windows that Pa had made, and they were glad they could see out. But they wished they could see snow.

Laura was anxious because Christmas was near, and Santa Claus and his reindeer could not travel without snow. Mary was afraid that, even if it snowed, Santa Claus could not find them, so far away in Indian Territory. When they asked Ma about this, she said she didn't know.

"What day is it?" they asked her, anxiously. "How many more days till Christmas?" And they counted off the days on their fingers, till there was only one more day left.

Rain was still falling that morning. There was not one crack in the grey sky. They felt almost sure there would be no Christmas. Still, they kept hoping.

Just before noon the light changed. The clouds broke and drifted apart, shining white in a clear blue sky. The sun shone, birds sang, and thousands of drops of water sparkled on the grasses. But when Ma opened the door to let in the fresh, cold air, they heard the creek roaring.

They had not thought about the creek. Now they knew they would have no Christmas, because Santa Claus could not cross that roaring creek.

Pa came in, bringing a big fat turkey. If it weighed less than twenty pounds, he said, he'd eat it, feathers and all. He asked Laura, "How's that for a Christmas dinner? Think you can manage one of those drumsticks?"

She said, yes, she could. But she was sober. Then Mary asked him if the creek was going down, and he said it was still rising.

Ma said it was too bad. She hated to think of Mr Edwards eating his bachelor cooking all alone on Christmas day. Mr Edwards had been asked to eat Christmas dinner with them, but Pa shook his head and said a man would risk his neck, trying to cross that creek now.

"No," he said. "That current's too strong. We'll just have to make up our minds that Edwards won't be here tomorrow."

Of course that meant that Santa Claus could not come, either.

Laura and Mary tried not to mind too much. They watched Ma dress the wild turkey, and it was a very fat turkey. They were lucky little girls, to have a good house to live in, and a warm fire to sit by, and such a turkey for their Christmas dinner. Ma said so, and it was true. Ma said it was too bad that Santa Claus couldn't come this year, but they were such good girls that he hadn't forgotten them; he would surely come next year.

Still, they were not happy.

After supper that night they washed their hands and faces, buttoned their red-flannel nightgowns, tied their nightcap strings, and soberly said their prayers. They lay down in bed and pulled the covers up. It did not seem at all like Christmas time.

Pa and Ma sat silent by the fire. After a while Ma asked why Pa didn't play the fiddle, and he said, "I don't seem to have the heart to, Caroline."

After a longer while, Ma suddenly stood up.

"I'm going to hang up your stockings, girls," she said. "Maybe something will happen."

Laura's heart jumped. But then she thought again of the creek and she knew nothing could happen.

Ma took one of Mary's clean stockings and one of Laura's, and she hung them from the mantelshelf, on either side of the fireplace. Laura and Mary watched her over the edge of the bed-covers.

"Now go to sleep," Ma said, kissing them good night. "Morning will come quicker if you're asleep."

She sat down again by the fire and Laura almost went to sleep. She woke up a little when she heard Pa say: "You've only made it worse, Caroline." And she thought she heard Ma say: "No, Charles. There's the white sugar." But perhaps she was dreaming.

Then she heard Jack growl savagely. The door-latch rattled and someone said, "Ingalls! Ingalls!" Pa was stirring up the fire, and when he opened the door Laura saw that it was morning. The outdoors was grey.

"Great fish-hooks, Edwards! Come in, man! What's happened?" Pa exclaimed.

Laura saw the stockings limply dangling, and she scrooged her shut eyes into the pillow. She heard Pa piling wood on the fire, and she heard Mr Edwards say he had carried his clothes on his head when he swam the creek. His teeth rattled and his voice quivered. He would be all right, he said, as soon as he got warm.

"It was too big a risk, Edwards," Pa said. "We're glad you're here, but that was too big a risk for a Christmas dinner."

"Your little ones had to have a Christmas," Mr Edwards replied. "No creek could stop me, after I fetched them their gifts from Independence."

Laura sat straight up in bed. "Did you see Santa Claus?" she shouted.

"I sure did," Mr Edwards said.

"Where? When? What did he look like? What did he say? Did he really give you something for us?" Mary and Laura cried.

"Wait, wait a minute!" Mr Edwards laughed. And Ma said she would put the presents in the stockings, as Santa Claus intended. She said they mustn't look.

Mr Edwards came and sat on the floor by their bed, and he answered every question they asked him. They honestly tried not to look at Ma, and they didn't quite see what she was doing.

When he saw the creek rising, Mr Edwards said, he had known that Santa Claus could not get across it. ("But you crossed it," Laura said. "Yes," Mr Edwards replied, "but Santa Claus is too old and fat. He couldn't make it, where a long, lean razor-back like me could do so.") And Mr Edwards reasoned that if Santa Claus couldn't cross the creek, likely he would come no farther south than Independence. Why should he come forty miles across the prairie, only to be turned back? Of course he wouldn't do that!

So Mr Edwards had walked to Independence. ("In the rain?" Mary asked. Mr Edwards said he wore his rubber coat.) And there, coming down the street in Independence, he had met Santa Claus. ("In the daytime?" Laura asked. She hadn't thought that anyone could see Santa Claus in the daytime. No, Mr Edwards said; it was night, but light shone out across the street from the saloons.)

Well, the first thing Santa Claus said was, "Hello, Edwards!" ("Did he know you?" Mary asked, and Laura asked, "How did you know he was really Santa Claus?" Mr Edwards said that Santa Claus knew everybody. And he had recognised Santa at once by his whiskers. Santa Claus had the longest, thickest, whitest set of whiskers west of the Mississippi.)

So Santa Claus said, "Hello, Edwards! Last time I saw you you were sleeping on a corn-shuck bed in Tennessee." And Mr Edwards well remembered the little pair of

red-yarn mittens that Santa Claus had left for him that time.

Then Santa Claus said: "I understand you're living now down along the Verdigris River. Have you ever met up, down yonder, with two little young girls named Mary and Laura?"

"I surely am acquainted with them," Mr Edwards replied.

"It rests heavy on my mind," said Santa Claus. "They are both of them sweet, pretty, good little young things, and I know they are expecting me. I surely do hate to disappoint two good little girls like them. Yet with the water up the way it is, I can't ever make it across that creek. I can figure no way whatsoever to get to their cabin this year. Edwards, would you do me the favour to fetch them their gifts this one time?"

"I'll do that, and with pleasure," Mr Edwards told him.

Then Santa Claus and Mr Edwards stepped across the street to the hitching-posts where the pack-mule was tied. ("Didn't he have his reindeer?" Laura asked. "You know he couldn't," Mary said. "There isn't any snow." "Exactly," said Mr Edwards. Santa Claus travelled with a pack-mule in the south-west.)

And Santa Claus uncinched the pack and looked through it, and he took out the presents for Mary and Laura.

"Oh, what are they?" Laura cried; but Mary asked, "Then what did he do?"

Then he shook hands with Mr Edwards, and he swung up on his fine bay horse. Santa Claus rode well, for a man of his weight and build. And he tucked his long, white whiskers under his bandana. "So long, Edwards," he said, and he rode away on the Fort Dodge trail, leading his pack-mule and whistling.

Laura and Mary were silent an instant, thinking of that.

Then Ma said, "You may look now, girls."

Something was shining bright in the top of Laura's stocking. She squealed and jumped out of bed. So did Mary, but Laura beat her to the fireplace. And the shining thing was a glittering new tin cup.

Mary had one exactly like it.

These new tin cups were their very own. Now they each had a cup to drink out of. Laura jumped up and down and shouted and laughed, but Mary stood still and looked with shining eyes at her own tin cup.

Then they plunged their hands into the stockings again. And they pulled out two long, long sticks of candy. It was peppermint candy, striped red and white. They looked and looked at that beautiful candy, and Laura licked her stick, just one lick. But Mary was not so greedy. She didn't take even one lick of her stick.

Those stockings weren't empty yet. Mary and Laura pulled out two small packages. They unwrapped them, and each found a little heart-shaped cake. Over their delicate brown tops was sprinkled white sugar. The sparkling grains lay like tiny drifts of snow.

The cakes were too pretty to eat. Mary and Laura just looked at them. But at last Laura turned hers over, and she nibbled a tiny nibble from underneath, where it wouldn't show. And the inside of that little cake was white!

It had been made of pure white flour, and sweetened with white sugar.

Laura and Mary never would have looked in their stockings again. The cups and the cakes and the candy were almost too much. They were too happy to speak. But Ma asked if they were sure the stockings were empty.

Then they put their arms down inside them, to make sure.

And in the very toe of each stocking was a shining bright, new penny!

They had never even thought of such a thing as having a penny. Think of having a whole penny for your very own. Think of having a cup and a cake and a stick *and* a penny.

There never had been such a Christmas.

Now, of course, right away Laura and Mary should have thanked Mr Edwards for bringing those lovely presents all the way from Independence. But they had forgotten all about Mr Edwards. They had even forgotten Santa Claus. In a minute they would have remembered, but before they did, Ma said gently, "Aren't you going to thank Mr Edwards?"

"Oh, thank you, Mr Edwards! Thank you!" they said, and they meant it with all their hearts. Pa shook Mr Edwards' hand, too, and shook it again. Pa and Ma and Mr Edwards acted as if they were almost crying, Laura didn't know why. So she gazed again at her beautiful presents.

She looked up again when Ma gasped. And Mr Edwards was taking sweet potatoes out of his pockets. He said they had helped to balance the package on his head when he swam across the creek. He thought Pa and Ma might like them, with the Christmas turkey.

There were nine sweet potatoes. Mr Edwards had brought them all the way from town, too. It was just too much. Pa said so. "It's too much, Edwards," he said. They never could thank him enough.

Mary and Laura were much too excited to eat breakfast. They drank the milk from their shining new cups, but they could not swallow the rabbit stew and the cornmeal mush.

"Don't make them, Charles," Ma said. "It will soon be dinner-time."

For Christmas dinner there was the tender, juicy, roasted turkey. There were the sweet potatoes, baked in the ashes and carefully wiped so that you could eat the good skins, too. There was a loaf of salt-rising bread made from the last of the white flour.

And after all that there were stewed dried blackberries and little cakes. But these little cakes were made with brown sugar and they did not have white sugar sprinkled over their tops.

Then Pa and Ma and Mr Edwards sat by the fire and talked about Christmas times back in Tennessee and up north in the Big Woods. But Mary and Laura looked at their beautiful cakes and played with their pennies and drank water out of their new cups. And little by little they licked and sucked their sticks of candy, till each stick was sharp-pointed on one end.

That was a happy Christmas.

OTHER PLACES,
OTHER WAYS

AUSTRALIA, 1769

Joseph Banks, *the great botanist, was twenty-four when he set out, in a vessel equipped at his own expense, with Captain Cook's* Endeavour *expedition round the world, including New Zealand and eastern Australia. In December 1769 they were off Cape Maria Van Diemen, north of Australia.*

24th December
Myself in a boat shooting in which I had good Success, killing chiefly several Gannets or Solan Geese, so like European ones that they are hardly distinguishable from them as it was the humor of the Ship to keep Christmas in the Old fashioned way it was resolved of them to make a Goose pye for to morrows dinner.

25th December, Christmas Day
Our Goose pye was eat with great approbation & in the Evening all hands were as drunk as our forefathers used to be upon like Occasion.

26th December
This Morn all heads ached with Yesterdays debauch...

PATAGONIA, 1833

The naturalist Charles Darwin *was twenty-four, and two years into his five-year voyage with* HMS Beagle *on its scientific survey of South American waters, when they were anchored off Port Desire, Patagonia, for Christmas, 1833.*

24th December

Wretched looking as the country is, it supports very many Guanacoes. By great good luck I shot one; it weighed without its entrails 170 pounds: so that we shall have fresh meat for all hands on Christmas day.

Christmas, 25th December

After dining in the Gun-room, the officers & almost every man in the ship went ashore. The Captain distributed prizes to the best runners, leapers, wrestlers. These Olympic games were very amusing; it was quite delightful to see with what school-boy eagerness the seamen enjoyed them: old men with long beards & young men without any were playing like so many children. Certainly a much better way of passing Christmas day than the usual one, of every seaman getting as drunk as he possibly can.

DEATH VALLEY, CALIFORNIA, 1849

In 1849 a group of pioneer prospectors and immigrants, called the Jayhawkers, were searching for a shortcut to California that avoided the high snowbound passes. They blundered tragically into the awesome 120-mile-long wastes of what they would later name Death Valley. Stranded, they burned their wagons and struggled forward on foot.

As the only woman, Julia Brier was greatly admired by her companions for her uncomplaining courage, but when, in Christmas 1898, aged eighty-four, she was interviewed by a San Francisco newspaper, it was the first time she had ever felt able to speak of their ordeal.

Mr Brier, our three boys, Columbus, John and Kirk, the oldest being nine years, and two young men, St John and Patrick, made up our "mess", as we called it.

We reached the top of the divide between Death and Ash Valleys and, oh, what a desolate country we looked down into. The next morning we started down. The men said they could see what looked like springs out in the valley. Mr Brier was always ahead to explore and find water, so I left with our three boys to help bring up the cattle. We expected to reach the springs in a few hours and the men pushed ahead. I was sick and weary, and the hope of a good camping place was all that kept me up. Poor little Kirk gave out and I carried him on my back, barely seeing where I was going, until he would say, "Mother, I can walk now." Poor little fellow! He would stumble on a little way over the salty marsh and sink down crying, "I can't go any further." Then I would carry him again, and soothe him as best I could.

Many times I felt I should faint, and as my strength departed I would sink on my knees. The boys would ask for water, but there was not a drop. Thus we staggered on over salty wastes, trying to keep the company in view and hoping at every step to come to the springs. Oh, such a day! If we had stopped I knew the men would come back at night for us, but I didn't want to be thought a drag or a hindrance.

Night came down and we lost all track of those ahead. I would get down on my knees and look in the starlight for the ox tracks and then we could stumble on. There was not a sound and I didn't know whether we would ever reach camp or not.

About midnight we came around a big rock and there was my husband at a small fire.

"Is this camp?" I asked.

"No, it's six miles farther," he said.

I was ready to drop and Kirk was almost unconscious, moaning for a drink. Mr Brier took him on his back and hastened to camp to save his little life. It was 3 o'clock Christmas morning when we reached the springs. I only wanted to sleep, but my husband said I must eat and drink or I would never wake up. Oh, such a horrible day and night.

...Music or singing? My, no. We were too far gone for that. Nobody spoke very much, but I knew we were all thinking of home back East and all the cheer and good things there. Men would sit looking into the fire or stand gazing away silently over the mountains, and it was easy to read their thoughts. Poor fellows! Having no other women there I felt lonesome at times, but I was glad, too, that no other was there to suffer.

The men killed an ox and we had a Christmas dinner of fresh meat, black coffee, and a very little bread. I had one small biscuit. You see, we were on short rations then and didn't know how long we would have to make provisions last...

...As the men gathered around the blazing campfire they asked Mr Brier to speak to them – to remind them of home – though they were thinking of home fast enough anyway. So he made them a speech. It was a solemn gathering in a strange place.

So ended, I believe, the first Christmas ever celebrated in Death Valley.

The next morning the company moved on over the sand to – nobody knew where.

Weeks later the starving survivors arrived at a ranch, and eventually reached Los Angeles.

THE ARCTIC, 1872

Captain George E. Tyson *was the Assistant Navigator of the* Polaris *on the American North Polar Expedition of 1871, seeking to attain the position of the North Pole. The voyage was beset with disagreements, indiscipline and the mysterious death of Captain Hall, but by the second year, the ship had gone further north than any before and, in Tyson's overruled opinion, could and should have gone even further.*

On 15th October, 1872, in her winter quarters, it was mistakenly reported that she had sprung a leak; supplies were being unloaded on to a floe that night when, in a great storm, the ice exploded and the ship broke away from the floe. To the horror of those abandoned – nineteen people, including four Eskimos and their five children – she never returned.

The floe was originally four miles wide, but soon broke into pieces of only a few yards; in the next five months it repeatedly re-formed and broke, drifted and froze again. Miraculously – though largely due to Tyson – when they were finally rescued on 1st May, 1873, no one had died nor even been seriously ill!

Angry and bitter, but determined they should survive to "tell the truth of the doings on the Polaris", *Captain Tyson managed to keep a journal of their ordeal on carefully hoarded scraps of paper. But a Naval Board of Inquiry never satisfactorily unravelled the mysteries and suspicions surrounding this voyage.*

22nd December

We have turned the darkest point of our tedious night, and it is cheering to think that the sun, instead of going away from, is coming toward us, though he is not yet visible. The shortest and darkest day has gone, and I am thankful. Friends at home are now preparing for Christmas, and so are we too. Out of our destitution we have still reserved something with which to keep in remembrance the blessed Christmas-time.

23rd, 24th December

Strong northerly winds. Both nights there was quite a brilliant aurora; it seems to come timely to lighten up our Christmas-eve. We shall have a slight addition to our rations to-morrow, and a slight change of diet too. All of our hams were used up about a month ago, except one; this we determined to save to celebrate our Christmas. It will be but a small portion for each, but it will be a change, and mark the day. It is not very cold – about zero.

Christmas-day!

All the civilised world rejoicing over the anniversary of our Saviour's birth – and well they may; but, though we are out of the civilised world, and in a world of ice, storms, cold, and threatening starvation, we are still trying to rejoice too. We know and feel that God has not forgotten us, that we are his children still, and that he watches over us here, as well as over those who dwell in safety in the cities and in secure country homes. He is trying us by a peculiar providence indeed, but he has not deserted us. We will praise his name forever.

It is now 12 noon, and the twilight grows a little clearer. I have just finished breakfast. We breakfast late because we only have two meals a day, and the day is better so divided. My Christmas breakfast consisted of four ounces of bread, and two and a half ounces of pemmican warmed over the lamp. Some of the men call this "soup", and some call it "tea". This is a full ounce over the usual allowance of bread. Even that additional morsel of bread was a treat, and very welcome. Our Christmas dinner was gorgeous. We had each a small piece of frozen ham, two whole biscuits of hard bread, a few mouthfuls of dried apples, and also a few swallows of seals' blood!

The last of the ham, the last of the apples, and the last of our present supply of seals' blood! So ends our Christmas feast!

CAROL FOR THE LAST CHRISTMAS EVE

The first night, the first night,
    The night that Christ was born,
His mother looked in his eyes and saw
    Her maker in her son.

The twelfth night, the twelfth night,
    After Christ was born,
The Wise Men found the child and knew
    Their search had just begun.

Eleven thousand, two fifty nights,
    After Christ was born,
A dead man hung in the child's light
    And the sun went down at noon.

Six hundred thousand or thereabout nights,
    After Christ was born,
I look at you and you look at me
But the sky is too dark for us to see
    And the world waits for the sun.

But the last night, the last night,
    Since ever Christ was born,
What his mother knew will be known again,
And what was found by the Three Wise Men,
And the sun will rise and so may we,
    On the last morn, on Christmas Morn,
Umpteen hundred and eternity.

Norman Nicholson

A CAROL

The warmth of cows
    That chewed on hay
And cherubim
Protected Him
    As small He lay.

Chickens and sheep
    Knew He was there
Because all night
A holy light
    Suffused the air.

Darkness was long
    And the sun brief
When the Child arose
A man of sorrows
    And friend to grief.

Donald Hall

INNOCENT'S SONG

Who's that knocking on the window,
Who's that standing at the door,
What are all those presents
Lying on the kitchen floor?

Who is the smiling stranger
With hair as white as gin,
What is he doing with the children
And who could have let him in?

Why has he rubies on his fingers,
A cold, cold crown on his head,
Why, when he caws his carol,
Does the salty snow run red?

Why does he ferry my fireside
As a spider on a thread,
His fingers made of fuses
And his tongue of gingerbread?

Why does the world before him
Melt in a million suns,
Why do his yellow, yearning eyes
Burn like saffron buns?

Watch where he comes walking
Out of the Christmas flame,
Dancing, double-talking:

Herod is his name.

Charles Causley

CAROL

There was a Boy bedded in bracken
    Like to a sleeping snake all curled he lay
        On his thin navel turned this spinning sphere
            Each feeble finger fetched seven suns away
            He was not dropped in good-for-lambing weather
            He took no suck when shook buds sing together
            But he is come in cold-as-workhouse weather
                Poor as a Salford child.

John Short

CHRISTMAS IN BIAFRA (1969)

This sunken-eyed moment wobbling
down the rocky steepness on broken
bones slowly fearfully to hideous
concourse of gathering sorrows in the valley
would yet become in another year a lost
Christmas irretrievable in the heights
its exploding inferno transmuted
by cosmic distances to the peacefulness
of a cool twinkling star... To death-cells
of that moment came faraway sounds of other
men's carols floating on crackling waves
mocking us. With regret? Hope? Longing? None of
these, strangely, not even despair rather
distilling pure transcendental hate...

Beyond the hospital gate
the good nuns had set up a manger
of palms to house a fine plastercast
scene at Bethlehem. The Holy
Family was central, serene, the Child
Jesus plump wise-looking and rose-cheeked; one
of the magi in keeping with legend
a black Othello in sumptuous robes. Other
figures of men and angels stood
at well-appointed distances from
the heart of the divine miracle
and the usual cattle gazed on
in holy wonder...

Poorer than the poor worshippers
before her who had paid their homage
of pitiful offering with new aluminium
coins that few traders would take and
a frayed five-shilling note she only
crossed herself and prayed open-eyed. Her
infant son flat like a dead lizard
on her shoulder his arms and legs
cauterized by famine was a miracle
of its own kind. Large sunken eyes
stricken past boredom to a flat
unrecognised glueyiness moped faraway
motionless across her shoulder...

Now her adoration over
she turned him around and pointed
at those pretty figures of God
and angels and men and beasts –
a spectacle to stir the heart
of a child. But all he vouchsafed
was one slow deadpan look of total
unrecognition and he began again
to swivel his enormous head away
to mope as before at his empty distance.
She shrugged her shoulders, crossed
herself again and took him away.

Chinua Achebe

ADVENT 1955

The Advent wind begins to stir
With sea-like sounds in our Scotch fir,
It's dark at breakfast, dark at tea,
And in between we only see
Clouds hurrying across the sky
And rain-wet roads the wind blows dry
And branches bending to the gale
Against great skies all silver-pale.
The world seems travelling into space,
And travelling at a faster pace
Than in the leisured summer weather
When we and it sit out together,
For now we feel the world spin round
On some momentous journey bound –
Journey to what? to whom? to where?
The Advent bells call out "Prepare,
Your world is journeying to the birth
Of God made Man for us on earth."

And how, in fact, do we prepare
For the great day that waits us there –
The twenty-fifth day of December,
The birth of Christ? For some it means
An interchange of hunting scenes
On coloured cards. And I remember
Last year I sent out twenty yards,
Laid end to end, of Christmas cards
To people that I scarcely know –
They'd sent a card to me, and so
I had to send one back. Oh dear!
Is this a form of Christmas cheer?
Or is it, which is less surprising,
My pride gone in for advertising?
The only cards that really count
Are that extremely small amount
From real friends who keep in touch
And are not rich but love us much.
Some ways indeed are very odd
By which we hail the birth of God.

We raise the price of things in shops,
We give plain boxes fancy tops
And lines which traders cannot sell
Thus parcell'd go extremely well.
We dole out bribes we call a present
To those to whom we must be pleasant
For business reasons. Our defence is
These bribes are charged against expenses
And bring relief in Income Tax.
Enough of these unworthy cracks!
"The time draws near the birth of Christ",
A present that cannot be priced
Given two thousand years ago.
Yet if God had not given so
He still would be a distant stranger
And not the Baby in the manger.

John Betjeman (1906-1984)

The Savior must have been
A docile Gentleman –
To come so far so cold a Day
For little Fellowmen –

The Road to Bethlehem
Since He and I were Boys
Was leveled, but for that 'twould be
A rugged billion Miles –

Emily Dickinson (1830-1886)

CHRISTMAS AT THE SHELTER

There will be turkey. They will see to that.
Also some decorations for the tree:
some silver lengths of tinsel, scarlet tat,
even a star, and everything for free.

There was a time when I was Santa Claus,
the one the kids woke: "Look, Dad, look at this!"
I can remember carpets on the floors,
a fireside, a drink, a Christmas kiss,
my in-laws, indigestion and the Queen,
the blasted pudding never catching light,
more gift-wrapped hankies... but how long it's been
since any night has been a Silent Night.

In here, at least there's pillows for my head,
blankets to cover me. A proper bed.

Adèle Geras

AT NEWGRANGE

That sturdy tale, the climbing star,
The baby in the manger; the sun
That at the winter solstice, only then,
Slips through the dolmen's eye and lights
Artful chambers under rocky Meath;

The pale green hellebore,
The Christmas rose sterner than winter,
That prevails; say *hope, hope, hope*:
We are untrue, and superstitious, and in vain,
And saying hope in spite of everything.

Mary Sullivan

A FORTY-NINER CHRISTMAS

Hermann J. Sharmann *and his brother Jacob were small boys when their father left their new American home in Brooklyn to become a "forty-niner" in the California gold-rush. After a nine-month trail west, the family had lost almost everything before they established their first claim: Hermann's little sister had died, both parents were desperately weak and ill, and their house was a sheet of canvas with no furniture or beds. Sixty years later, he looks back.*

Brought up, as all Germans are, to regard Christmas as the great fête of the year... [Jacob and I] could not quite forego observing it, though there was little to rejoice in. We had saved a small quantity of gold dust as our share of the mining operations and we determined to spend it in celebrating.

My brother and I mounted the horse and started for Marysville [*the nearest town, ninety miles away*], riding foremost by turns.

"What you see that would make a welcome gift to the father and the mother?" my brother asked me. [*After great deliberations, they decided on something rare and tempting to eat.*] "Hermann," he cried. "Look at this. Canned peaches! Could anything be so delicious? Let us take the peaches." [The storekeeper] had but one can and regarded it as the most desirable thing in his stock.

After carefully wrapping up our prize and tying it firmly to Jacob's belt we mounted our horse again and started back. When dawn was breaking on Christmas morning we reached our camp by the river.

Our parents, lying on their blankets, answered our wishes of a "Merry Christmas" as cheerfully as they could. We kissed each other tenderly and talked for many hours of the former happy Christmas days we had spent back in our Brooklyn home. Jacob had brought with him a branch of pine which he had plucked on our homeward journey and he set this up in the earth that formed our floor.

"It is our Christmas tree," he said, and our good mother and father smiled through their tears. We found some bits of ribbon and cloth and all the little trinkets we had retained. With these my brother and I dressed our poor tree and we sat before it, trying to think that it was glorious, all covered with brilliant baubles, and loaded with

sweets and packets of good things.

We set about preparing the Christmas dinner with great secrecy and care. Jacob fried the flapjacks and made coffee. I mixed flour and water for the biscuits. We had not known salt since our arrival and we used a substitute which was commonly adopted among the forty-niners, gunpowder. It gave some little savour to the food, though I should scarcely recommend it as a condiment.

When everything was in readiness we set out an empty box between the pallets on which our parents lay. This was the table. We had two pails which served well enough for chairs for Jacob and myself. We brought in the hot meal on tin plates and arranged everything neatly where father and mother could reach without getting up. We both left the tent then and ran to where we had hidden the peaches. We opened the can with a knife and Jacob, the elder, had the honour of carrying it in.

We came in procession, Jacob leading and bearing the peaches like a butler bringing in the wassail bowl, I following. Jacob placed the can on the box with great dignity and looked at father and mother for applause. And then we had our crushing disappointment.

Neither of them could touch the delicacy. Nor could either taste the meal which we had arranged with so much pride. We both cried a little, but our mother comforted us and told us that we should eat the share for them...

That was our Christmas in California in '49. It was a time when we were close to bitterness and pain... Many happy Christmas days I have passed since then, but always there comes a moment, when my children and my grandchildren are about me, when I remember our sad celebration under the canvas roof on the banks of the Upper Feather River.

CHRISTMAS NIGHT OF '62

The wintry blast goes wailing by,
   The snow is falling overhead;
   I hear the lonely sentry's tread,
And distant watch-fires light the sky.

Dim forms go flitting through the gloom;
   The soldiers cluster round the blaze
   To talk of other Christmas days,
And softly speak of home and home.

My sabre swinging overhead
   Gleams in the watch-fire's fitful glow,
   While fiercely drives the blinding snow,
And memory leads me to the dead.

My thoughts go wandering to and fro,
   Vibrating 'twixt the Now and Then;
   I see the low-browed home again,
The old hall wreathed in mistletoe.

And sweetly from the far-off years
   Comes borne the laughter faint and low,
   The voices of the Long Ago!
My eyes are wet with tender tears.

I feel again the mother-kiss,
   I see again the glad surprise
   That lightened up the tranquil eyes
And brimmed them o'er with tears of bliss,

As, rushing from the old hall-door,
    She fondly clasped her wayward boy –
    Her face all radiant with joy
She felt to see him home once more.

My sabre swinging on the bough
    Gleams in the watch-fire's fitful glow,
    While fiercely drives the blinding snow
Aslant upon my saddened brow.

Those cherished faces all are gone!
    Asleep within the quiet graves
    Where lies the snow in drifting waves –
And I am sitting here alone.

There's not a comrade here to-night
    But knows that loved ones far away
    On bended knees this night will pray:
"God bring our darling from the fight."

But there are none to wish me back,
    For me no yearning prayers arise.
    The lips are mute and closed the eyes –
My home is in the bivouac.

William Gordon McCabe
In the Army of Northern Virginia

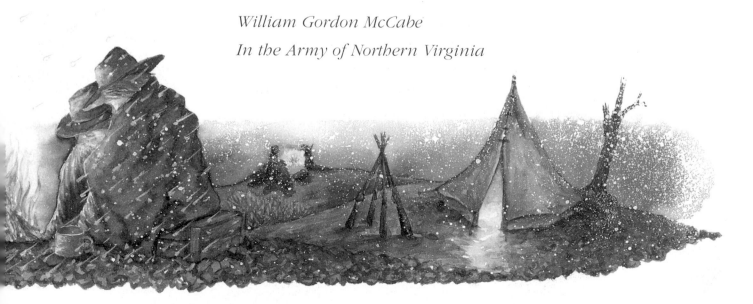

AN INDOMITABLE NURSE

In 1914 Sarah Macnaughtan *was at the Belgian front, running a soup kitchen at the Furnes field station and in charge of hospital orderlies, treating the wounded of all nationalities.*

25th December

My Christmas Day began at midnight, when I walked home through the moonlit empty streets of Furnes. At 2 a.m. the guns began to roar, and roared all night. They say the Allies are making an attack.

I got up early and went to church in the untidy school-room at the hospital, which is called the nurses' sitting-room. Mr Streatfield had arranged a little altar, which was quite nice, and had set some chairs in an orderly row. As much as in him lay – from the altar linen to the white artificial flowers in the vases – all was as decent as could be and there were candles and a cross. We were quite a small congregation, but another service had been held earlier, and the wounded heard Mass in their ward at 6 a.m. The priests put up an altar there, and I believe the singing was excellent. Inside we prayed for peace, and outside the guns went on firing. Prince Alexander of Teck came to our service – a big soldierly figure in the bare room.

After breakfast I went to the soup-kitchen at the station, as usual, then home – *i.e.*, to the hospital to lunch. At 3.15 came a sort of evensong with hymns, and then we went to the civil hospital, where there was a Christmas tree for all the Belgian refugee children. Anything more touching I never saw, and to be with them made one blind with tears. One tiny mite, with her head in bandages, and a little black shawl on, was introduced to me as "une blessée, madame." Another little boy in the hospital is always spoken of gravely as "the civilian".

Every man, woman and child got a treat or a present or a good dinner. The wounded had turkey, and all they could eat, and the children got toys and sweets off the tree. I suppose these children are not much accustomed to presents, for their delight was almost too much for them. I have never seen such excitement! Poor mites! Without homes or money, and with their relations often lost – yet little boys were gibbering over their toys, and little girls clung to big parcels, and squeaked dolls or blew trumpets. The bigger children had rather good voices, and all sang our National Anthem in English. "God save our nobbler King" – the accent was quaint, but the children sang lustily.

We had finished, and were waiting for our own Christmas dinner when shells began to fly. One came whizzing past Mr Streatfield's store-room as I stood there with him. The next minute a little child in floods of tears came in, grasping her mother's bag, to say "Maman" had had her arm blown off. The child herself was covered with dust and dirt, and in the streets people were sheltering in doorways, and taking little runs for safety as soon as a shell had finished bursting. The bombardment lasted about an hour, and we all waited in the kitchen and listened to it. At such times, when everyone is rather strung up, someone always and continually lets things fall. A nun clattered down a pail, and Maurice the cook seemed to fling saucepan-lids on the floor.

About 8.15 the bombardment ceased, and we went in to a cheery dinner – soup, turkey and plum-pudding, with crackers and speeches. I believe no one would have guessed we had been a bit "on the stretch".

At 9.30 I went to the station. It was very melancholy. No one was there but myself. The fires were out, or smoking badly. Everyone had been scared to death by the shells, and talked of nothing else, whereas shells should be forgotten directly. I got things in order as soon as I could and the wounded in the train got their hot soup and coffee as usual, which was a satisfaction. Then I came home alone at midnight – keeping as near the houses as I could because of possible shells – and so to bed, very cold, and rather too inclined to think about home.

PEACE BREAKS OUT ON THE FRONT LINE

This is an extract from a long letter that Captain Sir Edward Hulse, *Scots Guards, wrote home from the Western Front in 1914. Three months later, March 1915, he was killed in action, aged twenty-five.*

My dearest Mother,

Just returned to billets again, after the most extraordinary Christmas in the trenches you could possibly imagine. Words fail me completely in trying to describe it, but here goes!

On the 23rd we took over the trenches in the ordinary manner, relieving the Grenadiers, and during the 24th the usual firing took place, and sniping was pretty brisk. We stood to arms as usual at 6.30 a.m. on the 25th, and I noticed that there was not much shooting; this gradually died down, and by 8 a.m. there was no shooting at all, except for a few shots on our left (Border Regt.). At 8.30 a.m. I was looking out, and saw four Germans leave their trenches and come towards us; I told two of my men to go and meet them, unarmed (as the Germans were unarmed) and to see that they did not pass the half-way line. We were 350-400 yards apart at this point. My fellows were not very keen, not knowing what was up. So I went out alone and met Barry, one of our ensigns, also coming out from another part of the line. By the time we got to them, they were three-quarters of the way over, and much too near our barbed wire, so I moved them back.

They were three private soldiers and a stretcher-bearer, and their spokesman started off by saying that he thought it only right to come over and

wish us a happy Christmas, and trusted us implicitly to keep the truce. He came from Suffolk, where he had left his best girl and a 3½hp motor bike! He told me that he could not get a letter to the girl, and wanted to send one through me. I made him write out a letter in front of me in English and I sent it off that night. I told him that she probably would not be a bit keen to see him again. We then entered a long discussion on every sort of thing. I was dressed in an old stocking-cap and a men's overcoat, and they took me for a corporal, a thing which I did not discourage, as I had an eye to going as near their lines as possible... I asked them what orders they had from their officers as to coming over to us, and they said none; they had just come over.

They protested that they had no feeling of enmity towards us at all, but that everything lay with their authorities, and that being soldiers they had to obey. I believe that they were speaking the truth when they said this, and that they never wished to fire a shot again. They said that, unless directly ordered, they were not going to shoot again until we did...

A German N.C.O. with the Iron Cross – gained, he told me, for conspicuous skill in sniping – started his fellows off on some marching tune. When they had done I set the note for "The Boys of Bonnie Scotland, where the heather and the bluebells grow", and so we went on, singing everything from "Good King Wenceslaus" down to the ordinary Tommies' song, and ended up with "Auld Lang Syne" which we all, English, Scots, Irish, Prussian, Wurtembergers, etc., joined in.

It was absolutely astounding, and if I had seen it on a cinematograph film should have sworn that it was faked!...

During the afternoon the same extraordinary scene was enacted between the lines, and one of the enemy told me that he was longing to get back to London: I assured him that "So was I."...

At 4.30 p.m. we agreed to keep in our respective trenches, and told them that the truce was ended. They persisted, however, in saying that they were not going to fire, and as George [*the commandant*] had told us not to unless they did, we prepared for a quiet night, but warned all sentries to be doubly on the alert.

During the day both sides had taken the opportunity of bringing up piles of wood, and straw, etc., which is generally only brought up with difficulty under fire. We improved our dug-outs, roofed in new ones and got a lot of very useful work done towards increasing our comfort. Directly it was dark, I got the whole of my Company on to improving and re-making our barbed-wire entanglements, all along my front, and had my scouts out in front of the working parties, to prevent any surprises; but not a shot was fired, and we finished off a real good obstacle unmolested.

They apparently treated our prisoners well, and did all they could for our wounded. [A particularly courteous officer] kept on pointing to our dead and saying, "Les Braves. C'est bien dommage."...

When George had heard of it he went down to that section and talked to the nice officer and gave him a scarf. That same evening a German orderly came to the half-way line, and brought a pair of warm, woolly gloves as a present in return for George.

The same night the Borderers and we were engaged in putting up big trestle obstacles, with barbed wire all over them and connecting them, and at this same point (namely, where we were only 85 yards apart) the Germans came out and sat on their parapet, and watched us doing it, although we had informed them that the truce was ended...

The same comic form of temporary truce continued on the 26th, and again at 4.30 p.m. I informed them that the truce was at an end. We had sent them over some plum-puddings, and they thanked us heartily for them and retired again, the only difference being that instead of all my men being out in the "no man's zone", one N.C.O. and two men only were allowed out, and the enemy therefore sent fewer.

THE BURMA-SIAM RAILWAY, 1943

A young Scot, Robert Hardie, *was a colonial medical officer serving with the Federated Malay States when Singapore fell to the Japanese in February 1942. He spent three years in Thailand in various prison camps and base hospitals on the infamous Burma-Siam railway. Although these were larger camps, where conditions were (comparatively!) better than in some of the most horrific, penalties for keeping a record were severe. A talented naturalist and artist as well, he used army message forms hidden in a thermos flask, and later, when searches were fiercer, buried them in a cemetery at Chungkai camp, where he recovered them after the Japanese surrender.*

24th December 1943

Work in this camp has been fairly light recently, and Japanese pressure has been relaxed. We are to have a whole holiday tomorrow (Christmas Day) and all sorts of preparations are in progress. There is to be a football match between officers and men, a "race meeting" on some rough sand and gravel on the river bank, and in the evening a pantomime on an improvised stage facing a high gravel and earth bank. Various strange beers have been brewed, and great efforts in the cooking line are rumoured. The Dutch officers are coming to our hut for a drink in the morning and we go to their party later.

26th December 1943

Yesterday, Christmas Day, was a very remarkable and enjoyable occasion. A great *tour de force* by the cooks, who had been saving things up over a long period, produced a wonderful series of meals in the hospital.

Breakfast, at nine, was rice porridge with lactogen milk; followed by a fried egg, some thick fried pork and fried sweet potatoes; also a tapioca flour roll with a piece of margarine and a good dollop of lime marmalade.

Lunch in the middle of the day was two fish rissoles, following a plate of veg-and-meat soup, two slices of cold beef, some vegetable marrow and some pickles of cucumber and Chinese radish. To wind up, a cup of tea with milk.

Dinner was a veg-and-meat soup; roast beef with fried sweet potatoes and pumpkin; for pudding, a baked ginger pudding and a sauce made with limes;

savoury, a sardine on a fried rice biscuit. Dessert, fresh sections of the citrus pomelo; finally coffee with milk.

This sounds as if we were living on the fat of the land. It is true our rations are much better than they were, and we get a certain amount of fresh vegetable. But actually the elaborate menu given above is based on quite a few extras – the Japs allowed us to kill specially for this occasion one pig and one of the cattle. The milk is part of the hospital supply (bought by ourselves) and only the hospital patients were given it. The eggs were bought by ourselves. The fat for frying is mostly purchased by us, not an issue by the Japs. The margarine was some we saved from an earlier Jap issue, to celebrate the completion of the line. The lime jam is made from limes and sugar specially bought by us. The pickles are just part of our ration, in vinegar. Some tins of fish, partly Jap issue, partly purchased, supplied some of the other items. The whole thing was very well done and, though it had involved a fairly heavy levy on our cash, it was worth it. Most of the patients in the hospital were able to enjoy the food. Our parties with the Dutch officers went off well. There was enough drink to produce quite a degree of conviviality, and there was some very hearty singing.

The men won the football match 5-2.

The horse race, with bookies, was passably amusing.

The pantomime *The Babes in Thailand* was a remarkable performance...

Singing continued far into the night and for a wonder did not lead to any trouble with the Nip guards. One must admit that the Nips allowed a considerable degree of latitude.

Altogether it was a quite remarkably fine celebration for a remote jungle camp miles from anywhere.

REMEMBERING SNOW

Today I think of a boy in the Transvaal
Spending his Christmas Day at the krantzes
Where the khaki drought of veld, cleft open,
Held festivals of water in a fern-green canyon.

We dived fork-naked into crystal pools,
Explored behind the maidenhair waterfalls,
Eating our Christmas pudding beneath the grace
Of feminine willows on the vivid grass.

My mother lured the pony with lumps of sugar;
We coaxed him into his creaking cat's cradle of leather,
My father, all that tawny homeward run,
Remembering snow as I remember sun.

R. N. Currey

CHRISTMAS IN MEXICAN CALIFORNIA

José Ramon Pico, the nephew of Pio Pico, the last Mexican governor of California, remembers how Christmas used to be for the rich Californios.

Christmas in California before the Americans came was a season when all the grown people had as much fun as the children do now. And the children had so much fun that they never got over it and ever after loved play and presents more than work and hard bargaining.

[The first week of December] commenced the preparations for the Fiesta del Cristo, La Noche Buena.

Chickens by the dozens were boiled and for days the Indians worked pounding parched corn in stone mortars; the rich meal was rolled around the tender chicken, and the whole was then wrapped with chillies in corn husks to be steamed. These, packed away in jars, would keep until wanted by reason of the quantity of red pepper in the seasoning.

All this time the Indians had been eating, eating, day and night; the Mahalas *[Indian women]* made bread of acorns, laurel nuts and horse chestnuts; baked beans and meats...

Mucha fiesta! There never had been such plenty until the padres came...

By Christmas there would sometimes be three hundred Indians at the mission of Santa Clara, and many whole families of our relatives and rancheros who lived adjacent would come... We made presents, though there was no Santa Claus then.

To the Indians we gave young beefs to kill for fresh meat and also red blankets and handkerchiefs. To the padre at the mission we gave such things as carne seca

[choice dried meat], peppers, sweet potatoes and sacks of beans to supply their kitchen, and big bundles of dry hides for them to use in making chairs and furniture...

On La Noche Buena at our hacienda there were always many families beside our own... We had much music – guitars of the Mexican and Spanish type, made with twelve strings of wire, and mandolins. After supper there was dancing in the patio, coffee and cigaritos on the veranda, and singing everywhere.

[The young men and women would ride after supper over the valley to the Mission Santa Clara.] Our horses were the best of the big herds that were attached to every rancho. The saddles, bridles and spurs were heavily covered with silver bullion ornaments, as in those times we put silver on our horses instead of on our dining tables... Riding out of the patio gate it was like a scene from the time of the Moors in Spain. As our horses snorted in the cold air they spun the rollers in their bits, making music that only the Spanish horseman knows...

Back to the hacienda again... into the patio, where fragrant coffee from Mexico, tortillas and tamales de las gallinas *[chicken]* were served steaming hot from the big fireplace in the kitchen. Though we danced until morning, there was not a sleepy eye in the house. When daylight came we went to our rooms or took siestas in the hammocks under the verandas and were ready for almuerzo *[lunch]* when the bell rang.

And so for a week our Christmas lasted.

BIG BANGS IN EL SALVADOR

In December 1985, the American journalist P. J. O'Rourke *was in strife-torn San Salvador.*

From the balcony of my room at the Sheraton, I could see the entire city. There were powder flashes and staccato bursts in every neighbourhood. Rockets whistled. Huge explosions illuminated the surrounding hills. A dozen blasts came inside the hotel compound itself. Bits of debris flew past my head. The brazen face of war? No, firecrackers.

Everybody in Latin America likes to set off firecrackers on Christmas Eve, but nobody likes it more than the Salvadorans. They have everything – cherry bombs, M80s, defingering little strings of one-inchers and items of ordnance that can turn a fifty-five gallon oil drum into a steel hula skirt. The largest have a warning printed on them, that they shouldn't be lit by drunks. I am no stranger to loud noise. I've been to a Mitch Ryder and the Detroit Wheels concert. I once dated a woman with two kids. But at midnight on Christmas Eve – with the windows shut, the air conditioner on, the TV turned up and the bathroom door closed – I couldn't hear myself sing "Wild Colonial Boy" in the shower. On Christmas Day I saw people raking their yards, gathering mounds of spent grey firecrackers as large as autumn leaf piles.

You'd think after six years of civil war and 464 years of civil unrest, more explosions would be the last thing the Salvadorans would want. Or, maybe, the thing they want most.

SANTA CLAUS IN OAXACA

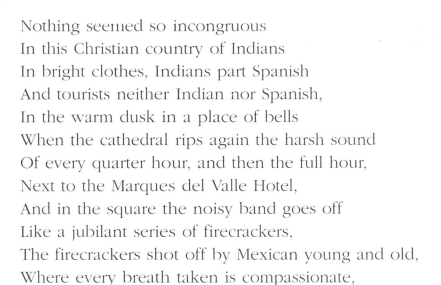

Nothing seemed so incongruous
In this Christian country of Indians
In bright clothes, Indians part Spanish
And tourists neither Indian nor Spanish,
In the warm dusk in a place of bells
When the cathedral rips again the harsh sound
Of every quarter hour, and then the full hour,
Next to the Marques del Valle Hotel,
And in the square the noisy band goes off
Like a jubilant series of firecrackers,
The firecrackers shot off by Mexican young and old,
Where every breath taken is compassionate,

Nothing seemed so incongruous
As to see Santa Claus in the hot lands
In red cotton garments, trimmed in white,
His bearded face impersonal but appealing,
Walk awkwardly through the square of Oaxaca
Followed by popping strings of boys and girls,
Mothers with babes mangered in red rebozos.
Where are you going, Santa Claus, walking?
Are you going to the ruins of ancient Mitla?
A gentle Zapotec explains the tombs of Mitla.
This Zapotec survives, but gone is the last fierce Aztec.
Are you hastening to see where the future would go?

Richard Eberhart

CHRISTMAS BREEZE

Auntie would say "Ah! Christmas breeze",
as the Norther leapt from the continent
across Caribbean seas,
across our hills
to herald Christmas,
ham boiling in the yard
plum pudding in the cloth
(Let three stones bear the pot;
and feed the hat-fanned fire).

This breeze in August cools a Summer's day
here in England
In December in Jamaica
we would have called it *cold*,
Cold Christmas Breeze,
fringing the hill tops with its tumble
of cloud, bringing in
imported apples, and dances
and rum (for older folk).
For us, some needed clothes, and a pair
of shoes squeezing every toe.

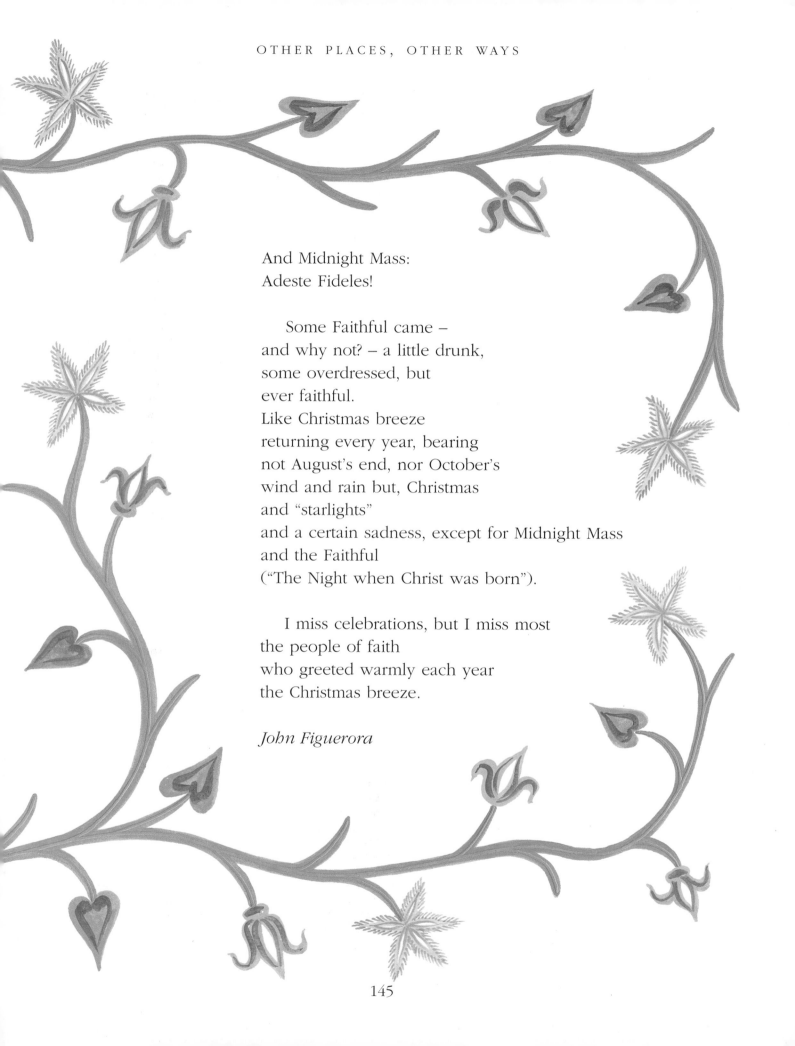

And Midnight Mass:
Adeste Fideles!

Some Faithful came –
and why not? – a little drunk,
some overdressed, but
ever faithful.
Like Christmas breeze
returning every year, bearing
not August's end, nor October's
wind and rain but, Christmas
and "starlights"
and a certain sadness, except for Midnight Mass
and the Faithful
("The Night when Christ was born").

I miss celebrations, but I miss most
the people of faith
who greeted warmly each year
the Christmas breeze.

John Figuerora

CHRISTMAS

In my country Christmas is
frangipani
jacaranda.
pohutukawa

is the flotsam holiday court in residence;
the king of the golden river
in swimming trunks, rubbed with sun oil,
saving the stupid who would drown outside the flags.

In my country Christmas is sun
is riches that never were rags
is plenty on the plate
is nothing for hunger who came unseen

too soon or too late;
is holiday blossom beach sea
is from me to you
is from you to me

is giving giving
in a torture of anxiety
panic of pohutukawa
jacaranda that has lost all joy.

In my country the feast
of Christmas is free;
we pay our highest price
for the lost joy
of the jacaranda tree.

Janet Frame

146

CELEBRATIONS IN THE DAYS OF CHARLES II

Samuel Pepys (1633-1703), an Admiralty official, wrote his classic diary in a secret shorthand, beginning in 1660. It described momentous events like the Fire of London and the Great Plague as well as his everyday personal concerns and the technical details of his work. He gave it up in 1669, after his wife died at the age of thirty, and his eyesight, a constant anxiety, finally failed.

25th December, 1662

(Christmas Day.) Had a pleasant walk to Whitehall, where I intended to have received the Communion with the family, but I came a little too late. So I walked up into the house, and spent my time looking over the pictures, particularly the ships in King Henry the VIII's voyage to Bullen *[Boulogne]*; marking the great difference between their build then and now.

By and by down to the chapel again, where Bishop Morley preached upon the song of the Angels, "Glory to God on high, on earth peace, and good will towards men." Methought he made but a poor sermon, but long; and, reprehending *[rebuking]* the mistaken jollity of the Court for the true joy that shall and ought to be on these days, he particularised concerning their excess in plays and gaming, saying that he whose office it is to keep the gamesters in order and within bounds serves but for a second rather in a duel, meaning the groom-porter. Upon which it was worth observing how far they are come from taking the reprehensions of a bishop seriously, that they all laugh in the chapel when he reflected on their ill actions and courses. He did much press us to joy in these public days of joy, and to hospitality; but one that stood by whispered in my ear that the Bishop do not spend one groat to the poor himself.

The sermon done, a good anthem followed with viols *[a stringed instrument played with a bow]* and the King came down to receive the sacrament. But I stayed not but... walked home again with great pleasure, and there dined by my wife's bedside with great content, having a mess *[serving]* of brave plum-porridge and a roasted pullet *[young hen]* for dinner; and I sent for a mince-pie abroad, my wife not being well to make any herself yet.

147

24th December, 1667

By coach to St. James's, it being about six at night; my design being to see the ceremonies, this night being the eve of Christmas, at the Queen's chapel. I got in almost up to the rail, and with a great deal of patience stayed from nine at night to two in the morning in a very great crowd; and there expected but found nothing extraordinary, there being nothing but a high mass. The Queen was there, and some ladies.

But Lord! what an odd thing it was for me to be in a crowd of people, here a footman, there a beggar, here a fine lady, there a zealous poor Papist *[Roman Catholic]*, and here a Protestant, two or three together, come to see the show. I was afraid of my pocket being picked very much. But all things very rich and beautiful; and I see the Papists have the wit, most of them, to bring cushions to kneel on, which I wanted *[lacked]*, and was mighty troubled to kneel.

All being done, I was sorry for my coming, and missing of what I expected, which was to have had a child born and dressed there *[a Nativity scene]*, and a great deal of do; but we broke up and nothing like it done... So took my coach, which waited, and through Covent Garden to set down two gentlemen and a lady, who came thither to see also, and did make mighty mirth in their talk of the folly of this *[Catholic]* religion.

Drank some burnt *[hot]* wine at the Rose Tavern door, while the constables came, and two or three bellmen *[night-watchmen who called out the hours]* went by.

25th December

Being a fine, light, moonshine morning, home round the city, and stopped and dropped money at five or six places, which I was the willinger to do, it being Christmas day, and so home, and there find my wife in bed, and Jane *[the cookmaid]* and the maid making pies. So I to bed. Rose about nine, and to church...

Wife and I alone at dinner – a good Christmas dinner. My wife reading to me... a strange story of spies, and worth reading indeed. In the evening comes Mr Pelling, and he sat and supped with us...

6th January, 1668
[After surviving a muddle that brought friends to dinner instead of supper, they all went to the theatre; afterwards] with much pleasure we into the house, and there fell to dancing, having extraordinary music, two violins, and a bass violin, theorbo *[rather like a lute or harp, fashionable at the time]*, four hands, the Duke of Buckingham's music, the best in town, sent me by Greeling, and there we set to dancing.

By and by... to a very good supper, and mighty merry, and good music playing; and after supper to dancing and singing till about twelve at night; and then we had a good sack posset *[a mixture of white wine, hot milk, sugar and spices]* for them, and an excellent *[Twelfth Night]* cake, cost me near 20s., of our Jane's making, which was cut into twenty pieces, there being by this time so many of our company, by the coming in of our neighbours, young men that could dance, hearing of our dancing...

And so to dancing again, and singing, with extraordinary great pleasure, till about two in the morning.

A DICKENSIAN CHRISTMAS: THE ORIGINAL ARTICLE

from The Making of Charles Dickens *by Christopher Hibbert*

Every Christmas Charles Dickens *took his children to a toy shop in Holborn to buy them presents, and would give marvellous parties.*

There was one memorable Christmas, in particular, the one after he finished the *Christmas Carol.* He had been utterly absorbed in the theme of that book, throwing himself into the writing of it with an enthusiasm that he had scarcely ever felt before, sharing the joys and sorrows of his characters as though they were his own. He had always been liable to do this, being as moved to tears by the tragedy of Little Nell, as to laughter by the comedy of his letters – George Putnam noticed in America how, when he was writing to his friends at home, Dickens's face would be "convulsed with laughter at his own fun". Now, over the *Christmas Carol,* he admitted that he "wept and laughed, and wept again, and excited himself in a most extraordinary manner in the composition; and thinking whereof he walked about the back streets of London fifteen and twenty miles many a night when all sober folks had gone to bed". He had finished it in less than two months, despite a great deal of unaccustomed rewriting, and then, again in his own words, "broke out like a madman".

And so at Christmas that year there were "such dinings, such dancings, such conjurings, such blind-man's-buffings, such theatregoings, such kissings-out of old years and kissings-in of new ones" as had ever taken place "in these parts before". And at a children's party at the Macready's house his excitement was feverish. He performed a country dance with Mrs Macready; he displayed his remarkable skill as a conjuror, producing a plum pudding from an empty saucepan and heating it up over a blazing fire in Clarkson Stanfield's hat, ("without damage to the lining"), changing a box of bran into a live guinea-pig. Jane Carlyle who was at the party and watched him exert himself until "the perspiration was pouring down", thought that, although he seemed *"drunk"* with his efforts, he was "the *best* conjuror" she had ever seen.

Thackeray was there, too, and Forster, and they were all "madder than ever" after supper with the "pulling of crackers, the drinking of champagne, and the making of speeches".

Then the dancing started and Forster seized Jane Carlyle round the waist and whirled her into the thick of it. "Oh for the love of heaven let me go," she cried out. "You are going to dash my brains out against the folding doors!" "Your *brains!*" he answered, "who cares about their brains *here? Let them go!*"

Another Christmas, Dickens had galloped round the floor "for two mortal hours" with Mrs Macready, after entertaining the children with a magic lantern and his conjuring tricks. Mamey and Katey had taught him the polka, and waking up the night before he had suddenly thought that he might have forgotten it, so he jumped out of bed and began hopping and prancing round the floor to remind himself of the step. At the party the next day, he went on dancing until everyone else was exhausted and gave in.

John Forster *was Dickens's closest friend and biographer;* William Macready, *another close friend, was a famous actor;* Jane Carlyle, *critic and letter writer, was the wife of* Thomas Carlyle, *the essayist and historian, and one of the most intellectually brilliant women of her time;* Thackeray, *of course, was a renowned novelist and humorist;* Clarkson Stanfield *was an Irish marine painter.* Mamey (Mary) *and* Katey (Kate) *were Dickens's young daughters.* A Christmas Carol *appeared in 1843.*

And, in later years, at his home, Gad's Hill, near Rochester in Kent:

Christmas was still a special time for him, not as a religious festival but as a time in which selfishness was transformed into charity, friends and families were reunited and all brought "back to the delusions of our childish days".

At Christmas time the house was sometimes so full that guests had to be boarded out in the Falstaff Inn over the way or in a nearby cottage; and their host would take the whole week off from his work to entertain them. On Christmas Day itself they would all sit round the big mahogany table in the dining-room, surrounded by the holly and ivy which covered the walls and dangled from the gas brackets; and when the flaming pudding came in they would greet it by clapping, and Dickens would give his traditional toast: "Here's to us all! God bless us!"

MOONLESS DARKNESS STANDS BETWEEN

Moonless darkness stands between.
Past, O Past, no more be seen!
But the Bethlehem star may lead me
To the sight of Him who freed me
From the self that I have been.
Make me pure, Lord: Thou art holy;
Make me meek, Lord: Thou wert lowly;
Now beginning, and alway:
Now begin, on Christmas Day.

Gerard Manley Hopkins (1844-1889)

INDEX OF TITLES & FIRST LINES

Titles are in *italics*. Where the title and the first line are the same, the first line only is listed.

INDEX OF AUTHORS

ACKNOWLEDGEMENTS

The publisher would like to thank the copyright holders for permission to reproduce the following copyright material. Every effort has been made to trace the ownership of all copyrighted material and to secure the necessary permission to reprint these selections. In the event of any question arising as to the use of any material, the editor and publisher, while expressing regret for any inadvertent error, will be happy to make the necesarry correction in future printings.

•Chinua Achebe: 'Christmas in Biafra' from *Beware Soul Brother* (Heinemann Educational Books). •John Betjeman: 'Advent 1955' from Uncollected Poems (John Murray (Publishers) Ltd). •Charles Causley:'Mistletoe', 'Innocent's Song' and 'At Nine of the Night I Opened My Door' from *Collected Poems* (Macmillan, 1975). Reprinted by permission of David Higham Associates. •Frances Chesterton: 'How Far to Bethlehem?' from *A Single Star* (Puffin, 1973). Reprinted by permission of A.P. Watt Ltd on behalf of The Royal Literary Fund. •Leonard Clark: 'Singing in the Streets' from *Wordspells* (Faber and Faber Ltd, 1988). •Beverly Cleary: 'Ramona and the Three Wise Persons' from *Ramona and her Father* (Hamish Hamilton, 1978). • R.N. Currey: 'Remembering Snow' from *Penguin Book of South African Verse* (Penguin, 1968). •Richard Eberhart: 'Santa Claus in Oaxaca' and 'Christmas Tree' from *Collected Poems 1930-76* (Chatto & Windus, 1976). •U. A. Fanthorpe: 'What the Donkey Saw' from *Poems for Christmas* (Peterloo Poets, 1981). •John Figuerora: 'Christmas Breeze' from *News From Babylon* (Chatto & Windus), copyright © John J. Figuerora •Janet Frame: 'Christmas' from *The Pocket Mirror* (Pegasus Press). •Roy Fuller: 'Christmas Day' from *Upright Downfall* (Oxford University Press, 1983). •Adèle Geras: 'Christmas at the Shelter', copyright © Adèle Geras. Reprinted by permission of the author. •Donald Hall: 'A Carol' from *The One Day and Poems 1947-90* (Carcanet, 1991). •Todd Hamilton: 'The Best Gift' reprinted by permission of the author. •Robert Hardie: 'The Burma-Siam Railway, 1943' from *The Secret Diary of Dr Robert Hardie 1942-45* (Imperial War Museum, 1983), copyright © Elspeth Hardie. •Thomas Hardy: 'The Oxen' from *Complete Poems* (Macmillan, 1978). •Christopher Hibbert: 'A Dickensian Christmas' excerpt from *The Making of Charles Dickens* (Longman, 1967). Reprinted by permission of Penguin Books Ltd. •Ted Hughes: 'Minstrel's Song' from *The Coming of the Kings* (Faber and Faber Ltd, 1974). •Norman Hunter: 'The Tree that Went Mad' from *The Peculiar Triumph of Professor Branestawm* (Bodley Head, 1970). •Tove Jansson: 'The Moomins Deal with Christmas' copyright © Tove Jansson. Reproduced by permission of the author. Originally published as 'The Christmas Tree' by Constable, 1958, translation © Marianne Turner. The Moomin illustrations on pages 52, 53, 54 and 56 are original illustrations by Tove Jansson, copyright © Tove Jansson. •Elizabeth Jennings: 'Afterthought' from *The Secret Brother* (Macmillan, 1969). •Laurie Lee: 'Christmas Landscape' from *The Bloom of Candles* , reprinted by permission of the Peters Fraser & Dunlop Group Ltd and 'Village Carols Between the Wars' from *Cider with Rosie* (Chatto and Windus). •Madeleine L'Engle: 'O Simplicitas' from *The Weather of the Heart* (Crosswicks, 1978). •C. Day Lewis: 'The Christmas Tree' from *Poems of C. Day Lewis 1925-72* (Cape/Hogarth Press, 1977). •John May: 'Six Things for Christmas' from *Messages,* ed. N. Lewis (Faber and Faber Ltd, 1985). Reprinted by permission of the author. •Gerda Mayer: 'Winter Poem' from *Winter* (Macdonald, 1987), copyright © Gerda Mayer. Reprinted by permission of the author. •A. A. Milne: 'King John's Christmas' from *Now We Are Six* (Methuen, 1927). •John Mole: 'The Waiting Game' from *Catching the Spider* (Blackie, 1990) and 'Ghosts from a Christmas Past' from *In and Out of the Apple* (Mandeville Press). Reprinted by permission of the author. •Jessie Eleanor Moore: 'The Story of the Star' from *Another Story Please!* (Nelson) •Krikor Naregatsi, 'The Christ Child' from *Anthology of Armenian Poetry* edited by Diana Derhovanessian and Marzbed Margossian. Copyright © 1978 by Columbia University Press. Reprinted with permission of the publisher. •Ogden Nash: 'I Remember Yule' and 'Epstein, Spare that Yule Log!' from *Verses from 1929 On* (Little, Brown), copyright © 1935 by Ogden Nash, renewed. Reprinted by permission of Curtis Brown, Ltd. •Judith Nicholls: 'Stable Song' from *Magic Mirror and other poems for children* (Faber and Faber Ltd). •Norman Nicholson: 'Carol for the Last Christmas Eve' (Faber and Faber Ltd). Reprinted with permission of David Higham Associates. •Leslie Norris: 'Mice in the Hay' from *Norris's Ark* (The Tidal Press, Portsmouth, New Hampshire, 1988). Reprinted by permission of the author. •P.J. O'Rourke: 'Big Bangs in El Salvador' from *Holidays in Hell* (Atlantic Monthly Press, 1988) •Alf Proysen: 'Mrs Pepperpot's Christmas' from *Mrs Pepperpot's Year*, translated by Marianne Helweg, (Hutchinson Children's, 1973). •John Rice: 'A Gift from the Star' •Michael Rosen: 'Christmas Dinner' from *Oxford Christmas Poems.* •Clive Sansom: 'The Innkeeper's Wife' from *The Witnesses* (Methuen). •John Short: 'Carol' from *The Oak and the Ash* (J. M. Dent). •James Stephens: 'A Singing in the Air' from *Christmas at Freelands* (Macmillan). •Mary Sullivan: 'At Newgrange' reproduced by permission of the author. •Dylan Thomas: 'Ghost Story' from *Quite Early One Morning* (Dent). •Dorothy Brown Thompson: 'Goodwill to Men'. •Alison Uttley: 'Tim Rabbit's Christmas Tree' from *The Adventures of No Ordinary Rabbit* (Faber and Faber Ltd, 1937). •Laura Ingalls Wilder: 'Mr Edwards Meets Santa Claus' from *Little House on the Prairie* (Methuen, 1937) •Kit Wright: 'The Wicked Singers' from *Rabbiting On* (HarperCollins Publishers, Ltd).